At Issue

Is the Mafia Still a Force in America?

Other books in the At Issue series:

Antidepressants

Are American Elections Fair?

Are Privacy Rights Being Violated?

Biological and Chemical Weapons

Child Labor and Sweatshops

Child Sexual Abuse

Creationism Versus Evolution

Does Advertising Promote Substance Abuse?

Does the World Hate the United States?

Do Infectious Diseases Pose a Serious Threat?

Do Nuclear Weapons Pose a Serious Threat?

Drug Testing

The Ethics of Capital Punishment

The Ethics of Euthanasia

The Ethics of Genetic Engineering

The Ethics of Human Cloning

Gay and Lesbian Families

Gay Marriage

Gene Therapy

How Can Domestic Violence Be Prevented?

How Does Religion Influence Politics?

How Should the World Respond to Natural Disasters?

Hurricane Katrina

Is Poverty a Serious Threat?

Legalizing Drugs

Prescription Drugs

Responding to the AIDS Epidemic

School Shootings

Steroids

What Causes Addiction?

At Issue

Is the Mafia Still a Force in America?

David M. Haugen, Book Editor

GREENHAVEN PRESS
An imprint of Thomson Gale, a part of The Thomson Corporation

Detroit • New York • San Francisco • San Diego • New Haven, Conn.
Waterville, Maine • London • Munich

© 2006 Thomson Gale, a part of The Thomson Corporation.

Thomson and Star Logo are trademarks and Gale and Greenhaven Press are registered trademarks used herein under license.

For more information, contact:
Greenhaven Press
27500 Drake Rd.
Farmington Hills, MI 48331-3535
Or you can visit our Internet site at http://www.gale.com

LIBRARY OF CONGRESS CATALOGING-IN-PUBLICATION DATA

Is the Mafia still a force in America? / David M. Haugen, book editor.
 p. cm. -- (At Issue)
 Includes bibliographical references and index.
 ISBN 0-7377-2402-1 (lib. bdg. : alk. paper) -- ISBN 0-7377-2403-X
(pbk. : alk. paper)
 1. Organized Crime--United States. 2. Mafia--United States. I.
Haugen, David M., 1969– II. At issue (San Diego, Calif.)
 HV6446.I7 2006
 364.106'0973--dc22
                                                    2005052816

Printed in the United States of America
10 9 8 7 6 5 4 3 2 1

Contents

Introduction 7

1. The New York Mob Is in Decline 14
   Jerry Capeci

2. The New York Mob Is Thriving 21
   David Usborne

3. The Chicago Mob Is Still Active 30
   Amanda Paulson

4. The Philadelphia Mafia Has Met Its Demise 35
   Kit R. Roane

5. The FBI Has the Mafia on the Run 39
   David E. Kaplan

6. Surveillance Technology Is Defeating Mob Rackets 43
   George Anastasia

7. Mobsters' Sons Are Becoming Suburban Hoods 55
   Mike McAlary

8. The Mafia Is Recruiting Sicilian Mobsters 67
   Clarence Walker

9. The Mafia Has Moved into White-Collar Crime 72
   CNN/Money

10. The Mafia Is Still a Force in Pop Culture 79
    George De Stefano

Organizations to Contact 87

Bibliography 91

Index 95

Introduction

Since the 1980s the American Mafia has been in decline. The FBI has systematically clamped down on mob operations, nabbing hundreds of members of major crime families and their associates. The well-known and resourceful heads of New York's five major Mafia families have been incarcerated, leaving less capable underlings in charge. Even worse for the crime syndicate, high ranking family members—possibly including the imprisoned patriarch, or don, of New York's Bonanno family, Joseph "Big Joey" Massino—are cooperating with authorities and undermining the code of *omerta*—or silence—that has supposedly safeguarded the Mafia's secrets and bonded its members to an "honorable" yet criminal coalition. The number of mobsters willing to break *omerta* and turn traitor against the organization that bred them signifies how poorly led and poorly united the Mafia is in the twenty-first century.

But it was not always so. From the 1930s to the 1960s, the Mafia was a well-tooled organization. It kept its activities underground and refrained from arousing the ire of the public. Throughout these early decades of the mob's rise, J. Edgar Hoover, the long-time head of the FBI, even denied the existence of organized crime. By the time Hoover did publicly acknowledge the existence of the criminal network in 1957, the Mafia was already wealthy, powerful, and entrenched in several American cities. It also had a quarter of a century of experience in racketeering, prostitution, gambling, loan-sharking, and murder. The organization has come a long way from its humble beginnings.

The Early Years of the Mafia

The Italian American Mafia began in the Sicilian neighborhoods of New York in the late 1910s and early 1920s. The Mafia was only one part of a vast underworld that included Jewish gangsters and Irish hoodlums—all vying for the bootlegging business that thrived during Prohibition. The Mafia made alliances or fought turf wars with these rival gangs throughout the decade. By the 1930s, though, the Italians and the Jews had come out on top. Through the work of men like Al Capone and Stefano Monastero, the mob had penetrated cities such as Chicago and Philadelphia and had taken the lion's share of criminal profits. The Italian gangsters also formed a commission of the five major New York Mafia "families" and Capone's Chicago network to lessen the in-fighting and focus on making money. The wealth generated from the Prohibition years encouraged the mob to expand their criminal activities to extortion and bookmaking. Local authorities were often ineffective at curbing the new tide of crime because many politicians and police officers were commonly in the pay of the criminals. Furthermore, since Hoover's FBI failed to take note of the mob's power and expansion, the Mafia grew almost unopposed throughout the 1950s.

The 1950s were the heyday of the mob. The Italian Mafia under various family heads and the Jewish factions under the New York criminal mastermind Meyer Lansky had worked together to build an organized crime syndicate that stretched from New York to Los Angeles. In the 1940s this network began investing in legitimate gambling casinos in Las Vegas. By the 1950s the gambling city became a favored vacation spot for celebrities and jet setters, and the healthy profits from the booming resorts provided the mob with a tidy income.

In Chicago, the Outfit, the name given to the local Mafia, was also running casinos—though illegal, underground ones—and a host of strip clubs. The Outfit also moved some of its operations to Las Vegas as well as to Havana, Cuba, during the 1950s. In other American cities the criminal syndicate continued to expand by mixing criminal enterprises with legitimate businesses. Nightclubs, construction industries, trade unions, and even government offices in twenty-six cities were tainted by connections to the mob.

All of this activity, however, was hushed by the family bosses who knew that publicity was not in their best interests. Unlike the flashy criminals such as Capone or even Benjamin "Bugsy" Siegel—who first brought the mob to Las Vegas in the late 1940s—the smart and powerful mob bosses of the 1950s stayed out of the public eye. Most, in fact, were unknown to law enforcement. This changed, however, in 1957, when state troopers in Apalachin, New York, accidentally stumbled upon a national convention of over one hundred Mafiosi. The quiet criminal summit ended in a panic as the Mafia heads and their lieutenants tried to flee from the police. Sixty-three were caught, including the heads of two New York crime families and eight other Mafia chiefs. Although the police had no cause to jail the men, their identities were made known, and the American public began to suspect that J. Edgar Hoover's assessment of organized crime was inaccurate. Pressured by Congress and state authorities, the FBI chief had to recant his views and began a nationwide intelligence gathering campaign against the mob. Relying on informants and wiretaps, federal agents soon learned the extent of the Mafia's involvement in crime, labor, and government.

The Mafia Under Attack

The 1960s proved to be the first rocky decade for the Mafia. Although Meyer Lansky's Jewish contingent was declining, and the Italian American Mafia would come to rule the criminal syndicate from then on, most of the twenty-six American Mafia families were now known to police and federal authorities, who began their attack in earnest. Attorney General Robert Kennedy went after corruption in the trade unions. Dedicated sheriffs in Chicago conducted numerous raids on underground casinos and strip clubs. In New York, the newspapers began running front page stories featuring the latest busts of mobsters. As if the outside attention were not enough, the Mafia was also racked by internal conflict in the 1960s. Strong-willed Joe Profaci, head of the New York Profaci (now Colombo) family, faced revolt from his own ranks when he failed to reward his hit men properly. For the first two years of the decade, bad feelings pervaded the Profaci family and nine members were killed in an internal power struggle. The bitter feud only subsided when Joe Profaci died of natural causes in 1962.

The feud that entangled New York's Bonanno crime family in the 1960s was not so neatly resolved, however. Joe Bonanno was an eager boss who supposedly tried to have the heads of two competing families—the Gambinos and the Luccheses—eliminated out of fears that the two men were conspiring to take over the Bonannos' lucrative operations. When the plot was exposed, Bonanno—nicknamed "Joe Bananas"—refused to answer a summons to a five-family summit meeting to explain his guilt or innocence. He was summarily stripped of his role as head of the Bonanno family, causing a split within the family as some members remained loyal to Bonanno while others sided with the newly appointed boss Gaspar DiGregorio. The so-called Banana War lasted from 1962 to 1969, when Joe Bonanno agreed to give up his claim to the family and retire to Arizona.

One year prior to the commencement of the Banana War, the mob was also faced with its first turncoat to speak publicly about the structure and activities of organized crime. Joe Valachi, a low-ranking hood of the New York Genovese family, broke the code of *omerta* and testified before a Senate committee about his role in murder and various other crimes for the Mafia, which he called "La Cosa Nostra," an Italian phrase translated as "Our Thing." Although Valachi's testimony was probably exaggerated and he spoke about aspects of the Mafia that he would have little knowledge of as a "street soldier," he did name key Mafia bosses and attest to the extent of Mafia crimes.

Authorities realized that rounding up minor players like Valachi would be nothing compared to ensnaring family bosses, but the bosses—who only orchestrated the Mafia's crimes but never soiled their hands—seemed untouchable. In 1970, however, Congress passed the Racketeer Influenced and Corrupt Organizations (RICO) Act to help federal law enforcement hold Mafia bosses—as heads of a criminal organization—liable for the acts of that organization. With the power of RICO and the help of numerous traitors who willingly implicated their bosses in order to get reduced sentences for their own criminal activities, federal authorities finally believed they had the one-two punch to knock the Mafia out.

The Mafia Faces Further Prosecution

Through the 1970s and 1980s, the Mafia's fortunes did decline. The casino gangsters in Las Vegas were bought out by legitimate businesses, and the rise of off-track betting cut into bookmaking profits nationwide. The mobsters also lost the support of many politicians during this time. Facing constant scrutiny from investigative, print and television journalists, local officials had to publicly maintain their reputations as civic-minded leaders. Thus, many were less likely to be bullied or paid off by the mob and more likely to commit themselves to eradicating criminal elements. Mafia ranks emptied—occasionally at the insistence of the bosses who wanted to lessen the number of potential informants. Law enforcement simply bided its time, building cases against Mafia bosses through the testimonies of whichever hoods were willing to plea-bargain.

In November 1986, the heads of New York's five families and three other bosses were convicted under RICO statutes for being members of the Mafia commission that ran organized crime. In less than three years, around twelve hundred

Mafiosi of all stripes were behind bars and facing long prison terms. The men who took over the families were just as vulnerable. The most famous mob boss to be indicted in the 1990s was John Gotti, the patriarch of New York's Gambino family. Gotti had earned the nickname of the "Teflon Don" because authorities could not get previous charges to stick. But in 1991, after being captured along with his underboss Salvatore Gravano for racketeering and conspiracy charges, Gotti's cohort turned on him and testified against the Teflon Don in exchange for witness protection. Gravano was, at that point, the highest ranking Mafioso to betray the cause and break *omerta*. His treason showed the public and the Mafia leadership that the structure of the organization was far from secure. One by one, the big bosses of the Mafia's families were incarcerated over succeeding years. Those who have taken over are known to law enforcement, and the authorities simply wait and compile enough evidence to bring those men down as well.

The Uncertain Fate of the Mafia

Meanwhile, the Mafia remains active. Several of its old, reliable sources of income—such as gambling—have dried up, but other, more modern crimes—such as stock and securities scams—have taken their place. The mob ranks have also shriveled. The Gambinos, once the strongest of the New York families, now have fewer than 200 members. Some families, like the Toccos of Detroit, can account for only 100 members. With less opportunity and fewer operatives, Mafia territories have shrunk, and larger, enterprising gangs such as the Russian Mafia have taken their place. Law enforcement in many cities regards the newcomers—who are more ruthless and have no internal code of conduct—to be more of a present threat than the Mafia. Yet the Mafia has not dissolved, and it has seven decades of experience to draw upon. Its hibernation—though partly imposed by relentless federal crackdowns—may just be another of its ploys to remain far enough out of the limelight to carry on its normal, criminal routines.

1

The New York Mob
Is in Decline

Jerry Capeci

A long-time reporter and author, Jerry Capeci is a prominent authority on the Mafia. His "Gang Land" column runs regularly in the New York Sun. He also manages a counterpart "Gang Land" Web site that catalogs nearly every piece of mob-related news. He is the author of The Complete Idiot's Guide to the Mafia *(2nd edition) and a host of articles for several major U.S. publications.*

New York's infamous "Five Families" that comprise the city's Mafia have all suffered setbacks since the late 1980s. The Gambino family, with the death of its leader, John Gotti, in 2002, has received the most attention, but the four other families—the Bonanno, the Colombo, the Genovese, and the Lucchese (sometimes spelled Luchese)—have each had their share of misfortunes. With their bosses jailed and their underlings facing convictions for various crimes, the Mafia families and their enterprises are in decline. In addition, the DeCavalcante family, New Jersey's main Mafia outgrowth, has also been sapped of its leadership by criminal prosecutions. As fast as new lieutenants are promoted to acting bosses for the East Coast Mafia, federal authorities indict them, reducing the ranks and leaving the mob enterprises in shambles.

From Gotti to Gigante, the names atop today's Mafia org charts are old ones. But the times have certainly changed for New York's biggest families—and not for the better. Mob expert Jerry Capeci, who writes the "Gang Land" column for the *New York Sun,* looks at the state of the four other clans in the city's infamous Five Families, plus the Newark-based DeCavalcantes. All have bookmaking, loan-sharking, and extortion rackets. The Genovese family and, to a lesser degree, the Luchese family (like the Gambinos) also have viable labor-racketeering endeavors that let them invest and launder their ill-gotten gains in "legitimate" industries. Every clan has declined of late, some more than others.

The Bonanno Family Loses Its Don

The Bonanno Family

    130 to 145 members

    Boss: Joseph Massino, 62

    Underboss: Vacant

    Consigliere [adviser, family counselor]: Vacant

Last-year [2004] was a bad one for the Bonanno family—probably the worst in its history. Its boss since 1991, Joseph Massino, was convicted of seven murders dating from the eighties, and the Feds decided to try to execute him for a 1999 mob hit. Two dozen family members and associates, including three capos [captains] he selected to coordinate things while he battled the law from prison, were all indicted and jailed on racketeering and murder charges. [In fall 2004] . . . Vincent "Vinny Gorgeous" Basciano, the capo he chose to replace the convicted trio and serve as acting boss, was himself socked with murder charges. Since November 19, Basciano, 45, has been awaiting trial at the same federal lockup in Sunset Park as his boss and the men he replaced. In the new millennium, more than 40 family wiseguys and associates have been convicted and imprisoned, including a former acting boss, Anthony Spero, 71. On top of all that, Joseph Massino, the Last

Don, a wiseguy who surely amassed millions during his decade on top, says he can't afford a lawyer and has told a federal judge that he needs a court-appointed attorney.

Every clan has declined of late, some more than others.

Meanwhile, Massino is expected to tap an old cohort, capo Anthony "Fat Anthony" Rabito, as his "street boss." On his mob résumé, Rabito, 70, has a drug rap, a few dead bodies, and a keen business sense, according to FBI documents. He has owned a bakery, a café, and several nightclubs, all on Manhattan's East Side. Unlike a Las Vegas business venture that failed—a New York–style pizzeria called Fat Anthony's—his local endeavors were said to be moneymakers.

Operating from Behind Bars

The Colombo Family

    75 to 85 members

    Boss: Carmine "Junior" Persico, 71

    Underboss: John "Jackie" DeRoss, 67

    Consigliere: Joel "Joe Waverly" Cacace, 63

    For nearly twenty years—since he was arrested on February 15, 1985—Carmine Persico has run the Colombo family from behind bars. Convicted of racketeering twice—once in the historic Commission trial, when he represented himself—Persico has guided his clan through a bloody two-year war that cost the lives of ten combatants and two bystanders. Housed in a federal prison in faraway Lompoc, California, he has maintained control through a string of acting bosses, including his college-educated son Alphonse, 50. In recent years, however, Alphonse, John "Jackie" DeRoss, Joel "Joe Waverly" Cacace, and Andrew Russo, 70, a Persico cousin who filled in as acting boss for a time, have themselves been convicted and jailed. . . . [In 2005], the family's "street boss" is Thomas

"Tommy Shots" Gioeli, 52, of Farmingdale. Gioeli was a staunch Persico ally during the 1991–93 war. He's had chronic back problems for decades, but they didn't deter his effort against rebels aligned with Victor "Little Vic" Orena. On March 27, 1992, he was wounded in a wild car chase–shootout in Brooklyn. "He's got a crew of shooters who haven't really gotten touched," says one police source. The last time Gioeli saw the inside of prison was in 1980, for robbery. A key factor for his strength has been his ability to bridge the gap that exists between mobsters who were shooting at each other a decade ago. His top aide, acting capo Paul "Paulie Guns" Bevacqua, was an Orena supporter, as was Cacace, who paid Tommy Shots the highest compliment in 2000. "If you need to see me, tell Tommy," he told then–Bonanno underboss Salvatore "Good Looking Sal" Vitale. "Talking to Tommy is just like talking to me."

A Dwindling Clan

The Genovese Family

   200 to 225 members

   Boss: Vincent "Chin" Gigante, 76

   Underboss: Venero "Benny Eggs" Mangano, 83 (Incarcerated)

   Consigliere: Vacant

The Genovese clan, long considered the Ivy League of organized crime, is the only family whose heir apparent and official boss seem to be one and the same. Vincent "Chin" Gigante took over around 1982. He's been in federal prison since 1997. The Oddfather, whose crazy-man strolls in Greenwich Village in his pajamas kept him out of prison for decades, is scheduled for release at age 82, in 2010—if he lives that long.

His genes give him a good shot. His brother Mario, believed by some to function as Chin's acting boss, is active at

81. Their mom, whose calls of "Cinzini" out her Greenwich Village apartment window gave Vincent his nickname, lived to 95.

Until then, he has a committee of three serving as his eyes and ears: Mario, who ended three years of supervised release in June following a 42-month term for labor racketeering, and two longtime allies who hail from his downtown, or West Side, base: Lawrence "Little Larry" Dentico, 81, and Dominick "Quiet Dom" Cirillo, 75.

"Mario is a gangster in his own right," says one law-enforcement expert. "He's Chin's blood-family connection. Larry and Quiet Dom are trustworthy old-timers who do his bidding with little fear of opposition from within or outside the family."

As Gigante told a prison guard who wondered if younger inmates were bothering him: "Nobody f— with me." Or his disciples.

Plagued by Convictions

The Luchese Family

> 120 to 130 members
>
> Boss: Vittorio "Vic" Amuso, 70
>
> Underboss: Vacant
>
> Consigliere: Vacant

Since 1991, the feds have convicted five Luchese leaders, including Vittorio "Vic" Amuso and acting bosses. Two stand-in leaders, Alphonse "Little Al" D'Arco and Joseph "Little Joe" Defede, became turncoats. Another, Louis "Louie Bagels" Daidone, is serving life for murder.

The fifth, Steven Crea, 57, is serving three years for labor racketeering and due out of federal prison in August 2006. Crea, 57, who operates several construction companies, is viewed as the likely successor to the jailed-for-life Amuso.

Currently, the Lucheses have a trio of veteran capos functioning as a ruling committee: Aniello "Neil" Migliore, 71; Joseph DiNapoli, 69; and Matthew Madonna, 69.

Migliore, who served briefly as underboss to Antonio "Tony Ducks" Corallo decades ago, "is the biggest influence on the street," says one law-enforcement official. "He's more equal than the others," says another investigator.

DiNapoli got out of federal prison in 1999 after 29 months for fraud and loan-sharking. Madonna was a major heroin trafficker who supplied notorious Harlem drug kingpin Leroy "Nicky" Barnes in the sixties and seventies. He was "made" following his release from federal prison in 1995, after serving twenty years for drug dealing.

An FBI Onslaught

The DeCavalcante Family

40 to 50 members

Boss: Giovanni "John" Riggi, 79

Underboss: Vacant

Consigliere: Vacant

[In 1999] . . . after decades as the ugly stepchildren of the New York mob, DeCavalcante mobsters thought they had finally achieved proper respect from the vaunted Five Families. They had killed a suspected informer for John Gotti and had joint rackets with New York wiseguys. As a crew of the Garden State gangsters drove to a sit-down with New York mobsters, they were taped by the FBI talking about their newfound status—a rise in fortunes that seemed to be reflected on TV.

"Hey, what's this f— thing, *Sopranos*. Is that supposed to be us?" asked soldier Joseph "Tin Ear" Sclafani.

"What characters. Great acting," responded capo Anthony Rotundo. Unlike Tony Soprano, the DeCavalcante leader has been in prison since 1990. In 2003, John Riggi pleaded guilty to ordering murders both before and after his incarceration, agreeing to take ten more years in prison. Since 1999, nearly three dozen wiseguys and wannabes, including the family's consigliere and seven capos, have bit the dust on racketeering, murder, and other charges.

The federal onslaught has been helpful for one old soldier, Joseph Miranda, whose family ties go back to patriarch Simone "Sam the Plumber" DeCavalcante. Decades ago, after Miranda robbed another wiseguy, Sam the Plumber spoke up for him at a sit-down and saved his life, according to FBI documents. Miranda, 81, a family loan shark, owns a bar on First Avenue. For years, he's been griping about not being promoted to capo. Recently, sources say, he jumped a few spots and was elevated to acting boss. He didn't have much competition, and he doesn't have much to lead, but, as one law-enforcement official says, "this week, he's the boss. Next week, who knows?"

2

The New York Mob
Is Thriving

David Usborne

David Usborne is the New York correspondent for the Independent, *a British newspaper. He has written many articles on New York life and culture, including a few pieces on the Mafia. He has also contributed articles to other U.S. newspapers.*

When John Gotti, the head of New York's Gambino crime family, died in 2002, New Yorkers had mixed feelings. While they were pleased that Gotti's death might herald the end of a major criminal syndicate, they were also saddened by the loss of such a colorful figure who gave the city a certain Mafioso allure. Gotti's brashness and vanity struck a chord with the tough New York spirit, and many in the city had worshipped him as a folk hero. New Yorkers need not be torn in their sympathies, however, since Gotti's death will not mark the Mafia's demise. Although Gotti's leadership will be sorely missed by the mob, New York's criminal rackets are still in operation and recovering from repeated attacks by city and federal law enforcement. The city's officials are quick to note that the mob has extensive networks and thousands of members, while law enforcement has a minimal number of officers and agents to combat the ever-present threat. And their job is made more difficult by the fact that New Yorkers are still drawn in by the Mafia's charm.

When it comes to the Mafia, the people of New York seem to want it both ways. They love it that the wise-

David Usborne, "The Family Business," *Independent*, June 21, 2002. Copyright © 2002 by Independent Newspapers (UK) Ltd. Reproduced by permission.

guys are still in their midst, and glory in reading of their latest adventures and feuds. Just witness the baroque extravagance of . . . [the] wake and funeral of former Gambino family head, John Gotti, who died of throat cancer in a Missouri prison [in June 2002]. . . . Yet when prosecutors announce their latest triumphs in shackling the Mob, its residents applaud.

This is not as nonsensical as it sounds. For 70 years, this city and its tabloid writers especially have romanticised the brutal world of the Cosa Nostra [the Mafia]. Its existence is part of what gives the city its cosmopolitan edge. Former mayor Rudolph Giuliani may have taken some of the grit out of its streets and sanitised Times Square, but at least New Yorkers still have proper gangsters.

Or do they? Gotti's death, combined with a series of high-level arrests, trials and convictions, has given rise to the once unthinkable suggestion that the Mob may finally have lost its grip on the Big Apple. "Mafia era passes", enthused the *Evening Standard* [a British newspaper] the other day, claiming that Gotti had been "the last Godfather" and giving credit to "another Italian-American . . . former mayor Rudy Giuliani" for wresting control of the streets from the Mobsters, who "one by one . . . were broken".

A Mythic but Very Real Organisation

Is it true? It would be nice to believe it; indeed, it is tempting to think that the spectre of the Mafia has always been more myth than reality, exploded in our imaginations by the Hollywood directors of films like *The Godfather* and *GoodFellas* or the writers of the TV hit *The Sopranos*. The stories of Mob's antics just seem too vaudevillian to be real. They were real enough, however. And the Mafia remains—at the very least—deeply soaked into New York's culture.

To realise how deeply, you only had to be present at the comic opera that was the farewell to Gotti. First there was the two-day wake at a Queens funeral home. As if from the central casting department, the Mobsters came to pay their obligatory respects. (Failure to show at the wake or the funeral was not considered a crime punishable by death. But absentees will have been unfavourably labelled as lowly punks by Gambino lieutenants.) Huge Italians beefed up with steroids and arrogance—looking, as Pete Hamill in the [London] *Daily News* put it, as if they had each swallowed a fire extinguisher—guarded the doors to keep reporters out.

The Mafia remains—at the very least—deeply soaked into New York's culture.

The funeral itself, under a grey morning mist, could have been scripted by Nicholas Pileggi, co-writer of *GoodFellas*. The over-the-top vulgarity was epitomised by the obscene floral tributes (not to mention the fawning tributes paid by some of the city's tabloid columnists). There was a martini glass made of flowers, a racehorse and a straight flush of playing cards. No fewer than 15 black Cadillacs tracked Gotti's hearse through the streets of Queens, the pavements five deep with gawkers. Another 80 cars of less pretentious marques made up the rest of the cortege. And the cops were everywhere, some conspicuous, others less so. Notes were taken as detectives looked to see who had showed, who was paying the most respects to whom and who seemed to have faded from centre-stage. Licence numbers were noted. Surveillance cameras mounted on city lamp posts just for the weekend watched also.

All this hoopla for a murderer and a hoodlum whose downfall was his braggadocio and thirst for fame. He favoured $2,000 (pounds 1,300) double-breasted suits and loved to swagger in public, even sauntering among tourists for his daily meetings with his lieutenants at the Ravenite Club in Little Italy. On one such day, he scoffed to his close associate,

Sammy "The Bull" Gravano—the underboss who would later testify against him, breaking his oath of omerta or silence—about the critics who said he should take a lower profile as head of the family.

"We don't have to run and hide," he boasted. "What're we afraid of? It ain't a crime to meet and get together. I'm not gonna be a back-door boss". He even used to talk about the possibility of the Feds using electronic equipment in the floors above the club to listen in. Which is just what they were doing. Gotti's vanity went even further than most know. We learned recently that he had to visit his barber every morning before going out to have his nose hairs snipped.

"He's a murderer, not a folk hero," noted US attorney Andrew Maloney in 1990, announcing the latest indictments against Gotti. What most interested the prosecutors was the gang-land killing in December 1985 on East 46th Street in Manhattan of Paul Castellano, the then-head of the Gambino clan. Castellano was arriving for dinner at Sparks Restaurant, when six gunmen in matching black raincoats emerged to gun them down. Castellano and his driver were killed instantly. The order to open fire was given by Gravano sitting in a car just half a block away. Beside him sat Gotti, who thereafter replaced Castellano as don. As the two victims lay on the street amid a scene of panic, Gravano and Gotti drove by to make sure the quarry was indeed dead.

Discerning the Truth About the Mob's Health

The city's contradictory view of the Mob is also fed by the media, which oscillate between declaring that it is on its last legs and then diving in with every column inch available when there is some new twist in the organised-crime saga to report. Wiseguy murders and Mafia trials have always sold newspapers, and still do. Rupert Murdoch's *New York Post* devoted 16 pages to the Gotti funeral on Sunday [June 16]. Wait a few weeks, however, and the same newspaper will once more be pronouncing on the impending demise of the once-mighty Mafia.

The truth about the health of the New York Mafia lies somewhere in the middle, of course. Much has happened [since 1992]..., most of it bad for the Mob. First, in 1992, came the conviction on racketeering and murder charges of Gotti, who had previously earned the nickname the "Teflon Don", because nothing thrown at him by prosecutors in three earlier trials had stuck. Even then, commentators declared that the reign of the five Mob families in New York—Gambino, Lucchese, Bonanno, Genovese and Colombo—that had started at the beginning of the Thirties was at last coming to a close.

And the pressure on the Mafia clans since has been relentless. Particularly ravaged has been the Gambinos'. Since Gotti's conviction, scores of its 200 members have been imprisoned or charged with varying crimes. Three of its acting bosses have also been convicted. Gotti's own family has been entirely decimated. His son, John Jr, named acting boss by his dad, was convicted of racketeering and illegal gambling in 1999 and will not be free until 2004. Gotti's brother, Peter Gotti, took over just a few months ago, but was charged with overseeing extortion and other rackets on the Brooklyn waterfront by prosecutors [in June 2002].... Another brother, Richard, and his son Richard Jr, were nabbed in the same sweep of arrests. There is no Gotti left to run the Gambino clan. Where once the Gambinos were reputed to be taking in about $1 [billion] ([British] pounds 700 [million]) a year, that figure has probably fallen now by more than half.

But the other families have suffered their own share of damage. The weapon used most often is the so-called RICO law, the Racketeering Influenced and Corrupt Organisations Act. During the Nineties it put numerous bosses in prison cells. The press conferences by prosecutors in Manhattan, Brooklyn and Queens announcing new arrests are still almost monthly events. The Brooklyn waterfront indictments this month named 17 Gambino associates. About 75 members of the Genovese clan were nabbed at the end of [2001] . . . accused of robberies, hijackings and assorted other criminal rackets. Others now in the care of the government include Alphonse "Allie Boy" Persico, the head of the Colombo family, his cousin, Frank Persico, and Vincent "The Chin" Gigante, the Genovese boss, who tried but finally failed to plead lunacy at successive trials. (He used to put on a convincing act by wandering the streets of Greenwich Village in a dressing gown mumbling to himself.)

[In May 2002] . . . one of the most storied Mob bosses, Joseph Bonanno, also died, but of natural causes, at the age of 97 in exile in Arizona. That said, the new head of the Bonannos is allegedly a reclusive figure called Joseph Massino, 58, who is free of any indictments and lives modestly in the Howard Beach neighbourhood of Queens. [He was later convicted of murder and racketeering and incarcerated in 2004.]

Much of the credit for the new ferocity of city prosecutors in going after the Mafia has gone to Mr Giuliani, who was a prosecutor himself before turning to politics and serving two terms as mayor. Indeed, his successful assaults on the Mob at the end of the Eighties and early Nineties assured him the publicity and the reputation for toughness that won him the mayor's office. But the authorities have been helped also by a degeneration of the old rules of the Mafia itself. As the judicial net has widened, associates have panicked and opted to help the government to escape long prison sentences themselves. Nobody broke the omerta bond of silence more spectacularly, of course, than Gravano.

Such a roster of death and incarceration would surely argue that the Mafia must indeed be tottering in the city. Not so, says one law-enforcement figure, who, though he prefers to remain anonymous on these pages, is a well-known veteran of the campaign against the Mob. Asked this week whether he buys the notion that the gangsters are a spent force in the city, he merely laughed. "Each family is still vibrant and powerful," he replied, "and they are each still inflicting economic and physical destruction on the inhabitants of New York City and the larger society. They are an ongoing domestic terrorist army".

Mob Ranks and Activities

It is worth pausing to study the structure of the families. First there is the boss. Even those in prison manage to run their clans' affairs to reasonable effect by making their decisions known through messengers. And acting bosses also mind the shop while they are "away". Beneath them are the skippers or "capos", who may number a handful or several handfuls, depending on the family. And the capos control individual crews, who are made up of all the other full members of the clan. They are variously known as "soldiers", "goodfellas", "wiseguys", "made men", "friends of ours" or "buttons". Latest estimates suggest that, even after all the recent carnage, the Gambinos have 200 members, the Colombos some 120, the Genoveses 250 and the Luccheses 120. Membership of the Bonanno family is much smaller, but the clan is considered to be strong, and the most disciplined of them all.

Yet even beyond the member crews, the families use the services of thousands of associates who are keen to help out with their criminal operations for the extra dollars but are not fully inducted into the families. They are the associates. So you begin to see what the authorities are up against. There may be some 700 made men operating in the city's five boroughs today. The army of associates could number about 7,000, however.

"Because you have arrested a John Gotti and taken out 10 or 20 of them, it doesn't mean there aren't thousands more out there," suggests the law-enforcement source. "Assume for a moment that the Mafia is a middle-sized company.

If the president falls ill, it doesn't stop functioning, the business still operates fully and the workers still make the product. In this case, they are still stealing the money".

And, indeed, they are. The bread and butter of the families remains loan-sharking—extending loans to individuals and businesses who can't raise cash elsewhere and then bleeding them for repayment. Drug dealing, hijackings, robberies and private gambling add to the coffers. And the Mob is still deeply involved in the unions, rubbish collection and in construction. The indictments this month against the Gambino members illustrated the degree to which unions on the city's piers are still subject to Mafia corruption and bullying.

The word was issued a few years ago that, at last, the Mafia's once-iron grip on construction in the city had been loosened. Loosened, but not dispatched entirely, it turns out.... [At the beginning of 2001], prosecutors fingered 38 Mafia figures and 11 companies for mixing the Mob with business. The indictments alleged that the Mafia's infiltration on scores of building projects, public and private, involving everything from schools, hotels and bridges, was adding 5 per cent to the cost of construction. That take is sometimes referred to as the "Mob tax" that must unavoidably be paid. Commonly, the money is extracted in return for a pledge for protection against other Mobsters muscling in. It is a scourge that still afflicts an industry that is worth around $30 billion (pounds 20 billion) a year and accounts for 7 per cent of New York City's economy. "You can't declare victory and walk away," Robert Morgenthau, the Manhattan District Attorney observed. "The fight against organised crime is far from over".

The pocket of just about every New Yorker is hurt in some way by the activities of the Mafia. Not long ago, the control exerted by the five families on the rubbish-collection business was costing taxpayers about $500 million (pounds 300 million) extra every year. On a more personal scale, the families in recent years have learnt to skim money from the telephone-card business. It is mostly the poor who buy these cards. Buy a 20-minute card in New York and chances are you will only get 14 minutes. The profits from the difference go to the gangsters. Small investors have also been hurt as the Mob has discovered new riches on Wall Street. [In 2000] . . . prosecutors arrested 120 people they linked to the Mafia on so-called "pump-and-dump" charges. The scheme, which all five of the clans operated with help from the Russian Mafia, involved the dissemination of false information about mostly obscure, hi-tech companies suggesting that their worth was far higher than in reality. After enough of the shares were sold, the remainder were dumped and the share price would collapse. Pressure, in the form of the threat of violence, was applied to numerous brokers to co-operate in the scams.

Feds Face an Ambivalent City

Many US cities have declared victory in ridding the streets of the Mob. But they are mostly small ones, where perhaps 10 FBI men were hunting down 15 gangsters. But in New York, it is very different. About 75 Federal agents work the Mafia beat in the city, day in, day out, but they are fishing not for tens of crooks, but for thousands.

The fight against organised crime is far from over.

And there is the other problem to contend with. As much as New York wants to be rid of the wiseguys, it is also deeply in love with them. The dons and the capos and the buttons do get respect. The kids see their wealth—most of the more senior Mafia figures who have been caught have been multi-millionaires—and want to live like them. So do the grown-ups. And in some neighbourhoods, it is dangerous to say anything bad about them. You might get knocked about. So it is easier to love them, because it is safer.

3

The Chicago Mob Is Still Active

Amanda Paulson

Amanda Paulson has written for the Christian Science Monitor *since 2000. In September 2003 she became the* Monitor's *Midwest bureau chief (centered in Chicago). She commonly writes on education and other social issues as well as regional politics.*

The recent indictment of fourteen major Chicago mobsters shows that the Mafia is still in operation despite law enforcement's successes in curtailing its power and influence. However, the mob no longer has the prestige it once had in Chicago during the mid-twentieth century; its networks have been systematically dismantled thanks to the Racketeer Influenced and Corrupt Organizations (RICO) Act of 1970, which helped make all persons connected to organized illegal activities liable to prosecution. Although the mob may be in decline in Chicago, it still has ongoing influence in criminal activities. Therefore, the FBI hopes that the recent arrests of major mob bosses will send the message that the law is still intent on bringing down the organization.

The indictment of 14 Chicago Mafia members might well be an episode of *The Sopranos*, complete with nicknames, "made" mobsters, family intrigue, crooked detectives, murders that go back decades, and a detailed explanation of a structure

Amanda Paulson, "With Chicago Arrests, Mafia Takes a Hit," *Christian Science Monitor,* vol. 97, April 27, 2005, p. 3. Copyright © 2005 by the Christian Science Publishing Society, www.csmonitor.com. All rights reserved. Reproduced by permission.

that includes capos, sotto capos, and a consigliere [bosses, underbosses, and advisers].

The indictment, announced Monday [April 25, 2005], charges the likes of Joseph "the Clown" Lombardo, Frank "Gumba" Saladino, and Paul "the Indian" Schiro with racketeering conspiracy and connects them with 18 previously unsolved murders dating back to 1970.

Along with being a colorful description of "The Chicago Outfit," the indictment is one of the biggest attacks yet on organized crime in the city of Al Capone—and a reminder that the Mafia, while weaker, still exists beyond the TV screen.

"They're alive and well," says Thomas Kirkpatrick, president of the Chicago Crime Commission, a citizens watchdog and advocacy group. The arrests, he says, are a big blow to the outfit. "I don't know that you can ever completely destroy it, but it certainly takes a major part of their leadership out and disrupts what's left in terms of people thinking they can trust each other."

Charges Point to Extensive Criminal Activity

The government has cracked down on organized crime since the late '70s, and has weakened groups that used to operate relatively openly. But such a far-reaching indictment, charging so many upper-echelon leaders with so many crimes, is extremely rare.

The Mafia, while weaker, still exists beyond the TV screen.

Since 1919, according to the Chicago Crime Commission, only 14 of 1,111 mob-related murders have been solved. This indictment would solve 18 more, including the much-publicized 1986 murder of Anthony "the Ant" Spilotro and his brother Michael, mob figures who were found buried in an Indiana cornfield and whose murders were portrayed in the movie *Casino*.

Beyond the murders, the charges paint a picture of mob-related activities that range from using extortion and threats to collect "juice loans" to running illegal gambling operations and collecting "street taxes."

Several of those indicted are "made" members of the Outfit—individuals who had committed murders for the organization or had otherwise proven themselves trustworthy, and who swore allegiance in a ceremony.

The FBI made numerous arrests in three states—Illinois, Florida, and Arizona—Monday [April 25, 2005], arresting James Marcello, the alleged boss of the Chicago mob, at his home. They discovered one alleged hit man, Frank "Gumba" Saladino, dead in a motel, apparently of natural causes. Two more—Joseph Lombardo, also known as "the Clown" or "Lumpy," and Frank "the German" Schweihs remained at large at the time of publication [April 2005]. Eleven of the defendants were charged with conspiracy, and two are retired Chicago police officers.

In the past three or four decades, "this is the largest indictment of its type in the Chicago area," says Frank Bochte, spokesperson for the Chicago FBI Office. "We're not fooling ourselves into thinking we've eliminated the problem, but we're hoping this sends a message that the FBI is still actively investigating these crimes."

A Still-Active Organization

While La Cosa Nostra [the Mafia] holds a celebrated place in the popular imagination, many see it as a relic of a bygone era. The Chicago arrests are a reminder of its existence, but also evidence that it has continued to weaken. Many of those charged are in their 60s or 70s, and the murders took place between 1970 and 1986. Other crimes, particularly those related to gambling, are much more recent.

"We've seen a tremendous drop-off in the number of mob-related homicides, but the tentacles of the mob still stretch into the illegal gambling industry in Chicago," says Mr. Bochte.

Since passage of the Racketeer Influenced and Corrupt Organizations Act (RICO) in 1970, federal agents have made significant crackdowns on organized crime in the US. The government's attack on the Mafia began in earnest in the late '70s, says James Jacobs, a law professor at New York University and author of *Busting the Mob*. Since then, the government has "made a lot of headway," he says. "They've sent hundreds of LCN [La Cosa Nostra] capos and bosses and soldiers to prison. It's been relentless, and it's occurred in every city where there are LCN members."

Gone are the days when politicians could openly dine with mob bosses, or when Chicago's First Ward was controlled by the Mafia, and everyone knew it. Back then, says Professor Jacobs, "they had hooks and influence in police departments, in City Hall, they were part of the power structure of the country."

J. Edgar Hoover, the former FBI chief, refused to devote any agency resources to fighting organized crime. But after his death in 1972, and with the advent of RICO—which made it possible to give significant prison sentences for mob activities—and the Federal Witness Protection Program, the government began a more concerted effort to wipe out organized crime. Federal moves have severely weakened it, and eliminated Mafia presence in at least a few cities, but it's been a tough battle—in part, says Jacobs, because so many arrests simply pave the way for internal promotions.

A Visible Message to the Mob

That's one reason officials are touting the Chicago arrests—for taking on so many people at once. As with most major attacks on the mob, it was made possible in part through alleged internal cooperation. According to the *Chicago Tribune,* Nicholas Calabrese, a "made" man who worked for South Side Street Crew (one of four such Chicago crews), was connected to the 1986 murder of John Fecarotta through evidence given by his nephew. He in turn cooperated with officials to give evidence against other members of his family.

The indictment "is remarkable for both the breadth of the murders charged and for naming the entire Chicago Outfit as a criminal enterprise under the anti-racketeering law," said US Attorney Patrick Fitzgerald in a statement. "After so many years, it lifts the veil of secrecy and exposes the violent underworld of organized crime."

4

The Philadelphia Mafia Has Met Its Demise

Kit R. Roane

Kit R. Roane is a senior editor with U.S. News & World Report. He is also a well-known journalist and foreign correspondent. He has covered domestic politics, American military operations in Iraq, and many issues related to New York City, his current home base.

Since the death of Mafia kingpin Angelo Bruno in 1980, the mob in Philadelphia has suffered from disorganization and internal rivalries. Federal authorities have caught and jailed a few of the most prominent mob bosses, and some of them have begun cooperating with the law to escape harsh punishments. The betrayals and the infighting signal the end of the Bruno era and the traditional adherence to the mob code of respect and honor, revealing that the once-powerful syndicate in Philadelphia is all but a faded memory. Law enforcement cannot rest easy, however; with the mob's presence dwindling in the city, the criminal element that has taken its place is likely to be just as dangerous and as well organized as the Mafia was in its heyday.

Philadelphia: The demise of the mob here—the end of the good life for Ralph, "Skinny Joey," and "The Crumb"—can be traced to March 21, 1980, the day "Docile Don" Angelo Bruno was killed in a hail of bullets. The Sicilian code of silence—omerta—died with him. Since then, internecine rivalries have left dozens of capos [captains] and soldiers [hitmen] dead or jailed and those still on the street so jittery that they're doing the once unheard-of: cooperating with the feds.

In recent years, similar turns have helped the Federal Bureau of Investigation break La Cosa Nostra's stranglehold in dozens of cities. But nowhere has the mob fallen so far as in the City of Brotherly Love, where former boss Ralph Natale has been chirping to the government for nearly a year. Natale is believed to be the highest-level mobster ever to cooperate with the government, and his revelations may put the final nail in the local Mafia's coffin. [In 2005 acting mob boss Joseph Massino became the highest-level turncoat.] That's the good news. The bad news: What comes next may be worse.

Nowhere has the mob fallen so far as in the City of Brotherly Love.

Even so, that does not diminish the import of the Feds' crackdown on the mob here, nor the singular accomplishment of reeling in Natale, who is seeking leniency for a host of alleged crimes, including seven murders. U.S. Attorney Michael Stiles is ecstatic about his good fortune; [in May 2000] . . . he indicted reputed acting mob boss Joseph "Skinny Joey" Merlino and 10 alleged associates on a raft of racketeering charges. And Stiles's luck just keeps getting better. In May, another reputed mob leader, Peter "The Crumb" Caprio, 70, decided to live up to his nickname and agreed to testify against Merlino. . . .

Times Have Changed

Bruno, the former "Docile Don," is probably rolling over in his grave. The proprietor of a chain of grocery stores, Bruno kept a lock on violence and shied away from dabbling in drugs or kidnapping in favor of loan-sharking, running numbers, and other gambling exploits. Under his leadership, the

Philly mob gained new prominence, forging ties with New York's Gambino crime family and stretching its reach into the gaming center of Atlantic City. "He gave people a code to live by, taught them respect and honor," says his 58-year-old daughter, Jeanne, standing by her South Philly rowhouse.

But times changed, as tough new racketeering laws put the squeeze on mob families and numbers rackets were hurt by legal gambling. Bruno was pressured by New York's Gambino and Genovese crime families for a bigger cut, and by members of his own crew to move into drugs. Bruno was killed shortly after the feds began asking him over for talks.

Then all hell broke loose. Lee Seglem of the New Jersey State Commission of Investigation says that between Bruno's death and Merlino's indictment at least 29 reputed mob figures in New Jersey and Philadelphia were murdered. They include one of Bruno's alleged killers, Antonio "Tony Bananas" Caponigro, who was found shot to death in a New Jersey field with money stuffed in his mouth, and Bruno's replacement, Phil "Chicken Man" Testa, who was blown up by a nail bomb. Snitches and prosecutors wore down the successive bosses. Natale, a ranking member of Atlantic City's Bartenders Union, took over the Philly mob after getting out of prison in 1994— but four years later he was back in, thanks to a parole violation.

Then came Merlino, "a young, flashy guy wearing strobe lights, saying 'I'm a mobster and proud of it,'" says Seglem. Merlino, 37, reflected the new mob, "sloppy guys who just wanted the veneer of being a gangster," says Celeste Morello, a mob historian who lives in South Philly. Merlino has maintained his innocence.

The Void Is Filled by Other Syndicates

As the mob's power has receded, other crime organizations have jumped into the breach, like Eastern European, Asian, and Latin American groups, as well as organized street gangs like the Bloods and motorcycle gangs like the Pagans. Experts say that Asian gangs involved in gambling, prostitution, and smuggling have established a base in Atlantic City and that Dominicans control much of the East Coast drug trade.

And so things are getting complicated. For one thing, the FBI doesn't have nearly the intelligence database on these groups that it has on the traditional mob. For another, the mob is now partnering with these groups. La Cosa Nostra families have been discovered working with Latin American organized-crime groups in drug schemes and with Russians on complicated tax swindles. What's different these days is that "there's no monopoly," says Temple University Prof. Nikos Passas, an organized-crime expert. "And that's going to keep law enforcement busy."

5

The FBI Has the Mafia on the Run

David E. Kaplan

David E. Kaplan is a chief investigative correspondent for U.S. News & World Report. Since the 1995 terrorist gassing of a To-kyo subway, Kaplan has written numerous articles on terrorism and homeland security. He is also the author of The Cult at the End of the World, *his account of the Tokyo gassing and the Aum Shinrikyo cult responsible for the tragedy.*

In the mid-twentieth century, the Mafia was a highly regimented, tight-knit criminal syndicate that had extensive influence in gambling rackets, union organization, and even manufacturing in many major American cities. By the 1980s, however, the Mafia's fortunes fell into decline. At that time, federal attorneys and the FBI initiated operations that disrupted mob activities and indicted many of its leaders. Key to their success was the implementation of the Racketeer Influenced and Corrupt Orga-nizations (RICO) Act, a set of statutes enacted in 1970 that gave authorities broad powers to target entire criminal enterprises for their connection to illegal operations. Using RICO, federal attor-neys successfully indicted Mafia kingpins for their connection to criminal activities even if they did not personally engage in those activities. Deprived of leadership, the major Mafia families in the United States suffered disorganization, and their powers have been curtailed. The Mafia, however, has proven resilient and is quite capable of learning how to outfox federal authorities even if, for now, those authorities have the upper hand.

For 40 years, [former FBI chief] J. Edgar Hoover denied that the Mafia even existed. Only in the 1960s, faced with Attorney General Bobby Kennedy's aggressive push to crack down on La Cosa Nostra [the Mafia], did the bureau finally take on organized crime. By then, the Mafia's influence extended from America's largest unions into tracking, construction, longshoring, waste disposal, gambling, and garment making. The Italian-American Mafia had grown into a multibillion-dollar syndicate of criminal enterprises run by 26 "families" nationwide.

Over the next 20 years, the FBI's anti-Mob efforts showed only modest progress. But starting in the mid-1980s, the bureau spearheaded an unprecedented assault on the Mafia, putting away two generations of godfathers on racketeering charges. Among the attorneys involved in those cutting-edge cases was a young federal prosecutor named Louis Freeh, who never lost his Mob-busting zeal. Whatever failures marked his tenure as FBI chief, Freeh pushed forward "the most significant organized crime prosecution effort in U.S. history," says Virginia Commonwealth University criminologist Jay Albanese.

Feds Keep the Pressure On

Key to the feds' success: their aggressive use of RICO statutes, under which entire criminal enterprises can be indicted, and stepped-up bugging of Mob cars, phones, and meeting places. Another breakthrough was cracking omerta—the Mafia's enduring code of silence. Faced with damning disclosures from wiretaps and the prospect of life in prison, top goodfellas have "flipped" to the prosecution's side. By keeping the pressure on, the feds have cut the number of active Mafia families from 22 in 1990 to just nine [in 2001], FBI officials told *U.S. News.* And while the number of full-fledged members has stayed at about 1,100, half of those wise guys are now in jail or inactive. Mob experts believe the Mafia's Commission—a ruling body of godfathers who mediate disputes—has not met since 1996. Once thriving Mafia families in Cleveland, Detroit, Kansas City, and Milwaukee are "down to two to three guys doing low-level scares," says Thomas Fuentes, chief of the bureau's Organized Crime Section. One result: Relative novices are now running the show. Officials are unclear if New York's Gambino family—once the nation's most powerful—even has a boss anymore.

The FBI can take well-earned credit for the Mafia's change in fortune. During the Freeh years, the feds piled up 274 convictions of Mob figures, including 20 top bosses. In [2001] ... alone, the FBI and New York City police arrested more than 70 people tied to New Jersey's DeCavalcante family, decimating its leadership. And in March [2001] came indictments of 48 alleged mobsters tied to New York's infamous five families.

The FBI can take well-earned credit for the Mafia's change in fortune.

Few law enforcement officials are willing to declare victory, though. They warn that the Mob has proved remarkably resilient and is moving into sophisticated white-collar crimes like stock swindles. "They're down but not out," says the FBI's Fuentes. "It's like a cancer in remission." And while the FBI still considers the Mafia the nation's top organized crime threat, other ethnic gangs have moved into the picture. Among them: Latin-American drug traffickers, Nigerian con artists, Chinese gambling bosses, and Russian mobsters. Unlike the U.S. Mafia, many of the new gangs are based overseas and are more fluid in structure. FBI officials concede they are badly in need of linguists and ethnic cops who can penetrate the new wave of mobsters.

Ironically, the FBI's Mob-busters may be victims of their own success. As the agency's budgets for counterterrorism and cybercrime have soared, funding for its Organized Crime Section has stayed largely static. So far, the good guys are winning, but, warns Albanese: "As the police get better, the bad guys get better too."

6

Surveillance Technology Is Defeating Mob Rackets

George Anastasia

Twice nominated for the Pulitzer Prize, George Anastasia is a reporter for the Philadelphia Inquirer *who focuses on mob-related news. He is also the author of several books including* The Goodfella Tapes *and* The Last Gangster: From Cop to Wiseguy to FBI Informant: Big Ron Previte and the Fall of the American Mob. *In the mid-1990s the Mafia allegedly marked Anastasia for elimination because of his investigative journalism on mob cases.*

In an era of computer microtechnology, the FBI is using the latest surveillance tools to crack down on Mafia rackets. In one instance, federal agents deciphered the password to a Philadelphia bookie's computerized gambling records by secretly placing a sugar-cube-sized keystroke recorder within the bookie's computer keyboard. Law enforcement claims that it needs such devices to keep up with criminals who are becoming more and more technologically sophisticated. Not everyone, however, agrees that such surveillance techniques are lawful. Lawyers for Nicky Scarfo, the mob-connected bookie indicted by the keystroke recorder, argue that these high-tech devices violate the accused's right to privacy—especially since no court order was obtained to install the device on Scarfo's computer. Although Scarfo was convicted for

George Anastasia, "Big Brother and the Bookie," *Mother Jones,* January/February 2002. Copyright © 2002 by the Foundation for National Progress. Reproduced by permission.

his bookmaking crimes, the issue of invasion of privacy is still undecided.

It started out as a run-of-the-mill bookmaking investigation in the Newark, New Jersey, area. Gambling and loan sharking. Sports bets on football, the colleges and pros. The usual stuff. The book was generating about $5 million a year in action. A decent-size business, it was said to be part of a Gambino crime-family operation.

This investigation had a little more sex appeal than most because one of the targets was the son of a jailed Mob boss. In certain underworld and law enforcement circles, the kid's pedigree carried a lot of weight. In effect, it made him seem more important than he really was, which might explain why the investigation eventually took the course that it did.

The kid is Nicodemo S. Scarfo. His father, Nicodemo D. Scarfo, also known as "Little Nicky," used to be the boss of the Philadelphia–South Jersey Mob. In his day, the elder Scarfo had a reputation for violence that was unrivaled. He's currently doing 69 years in a federal pen in Atlanta for racketeering charges that included 10 murders. The kid doesn't have that kind of rep. He's always been more interested in making money than making headlines.

The probe began in January 1999. The nuts and bolts of the case are pretty straightforward: A guy bets. A guy loses. A guy borrows money to pay off his debts. A guy pays 104 percent interest. Multiply that by a couple dozen guys and you've got a major book. All standard operating procedure in the underworld.

In this case, the feds zeroed in. Confiscated gambling records and wads of cash. Made arrests. Indictments followed. But on the way to what appeared to be a one-week trial, this standard, no-frills book making case turned into a story about Big Brotherism in the age of high technology, a clash between privacy rights and national security, a Mob case for the millennium.

Think of it as *The Sopranos* meets *The Matrix*. That is the only way to explain how young Nicky Scarfo, 36, with a curriculum vitae that includes surviving a Mob hit in a popular South Philadelphia restaurant in 1989 and serving nearly five years in jail for gambling and weapons offenses in the 1990s, has emerged as a high-tech poster boy for the Fourth Amendment.

Getting the Password

Scarfo was indicted in June 2000, following an 18-month investigation. What his lawyers learned as they began sifting through the evidence in preparation for trial was that the FBI investigation had hit a snag when the feds discovered that young Nicky was storing his gambling records—payoffs, bets, loan-sharking credits—on his computer. The tech-savvy mobster had encrypted these records using the latest privacy software, a program so powerful that even the FBI could not crack it—without the password.

How the feds got that password, and the records needed to make the gambling case, is the heart of the story. For in order to gain access to the files, the FBI used a sophisticated, highly classified monitoring device known as a keystroke recorder. The device, which may be no larger than a sugar cube, was planted in Scarfo's keyboard and allowed agents in a remote location to track the letters and numbers that Scarfo typed.

Scarfo's lawyers quickly claimed the feds should have obtained wiretap authorization before conducting that type of surveillance. The prosecutor in the case said the court-authorized search warrant that the FBI had used to plant the recorder was sufficient because the device was not intercepting electronic transmissions.

But when the defense pressed for a more detailed explanation of how the recorder worked, the government refused. They said the device was used primarily in high-tech national security investigations and that the technology was so top secret that "out of 27,000 FBI employees, there are fewer than 30 persons familiar with the underlying functionality" of the system.

Public disclosure of how the recorder worked, they added, could compromise "criminal and national security investigations, and . . . would possibly threaten the lives of rulers or other government agency personnel."

When federal Judge Nicholas Politan insisted he needed more detail to rule on a defense motion to suppress the evidence, the prosecution retreated behind the Classified Information Procedures Act (CIPA). To disclose details about the system, Assistant U.S. Attorney Ronald Wigler argued in another motion, would present a risk to national security and would violate CIPA, the law under which the technology had been classified. Not only is the technology classified, according to an FBI affidavit supporting Wigler's position, but the guidelines under which it was classified are also classified.

"It's the first case of its kind," said David L. Sobel, general counsel for the Electronic Privacy Information Center, a civil liberties watchdog group in Washington, D.C. "I'm a little surprised at the point at which it's escalated. . . . It's a question of whether the government is entitled to use technology so sensitive and so secret that it's not willing to disclose to a defendant how they gathered evidence. A defendant is entitled to know what was done during an investigation."

"They used a national security device to track a bookmaker," said Norris Gelman, one of Scarfo's lawyers. "What did they think, Osama bin Laden had a bet on the Detroit Lions?"

A More Sophisticated Criminal

Young Nicky Scarfo is no stranger to law enforcement. The FBI and the New Jersey State Police, it seems, have always been a part of his life. He grew up around his father's organization, which was based in Atlantic City at the dawn of the

New Jersey casino gambling era in the late 1970s. One of three sons of the Mob boss, he is the only one to follow in his father's footsteps, albeit on his own, decidedly 1990s terms.

The elder Scarfo was in many ways a throwback to a more violent Mob era. During his bloody run as Mob boss from 1981 through 1987, two dozen Philadelphia-area gangsters turned up dead, at least 10 on orders of the dark-haired, diminutive—Scarfo Sr. stands about 5 foot 5—Mafia don.

His son and namesake—taller, stockier, with blue eyes and light-brown hair—is more sophisticated. Likes the business end of the business. Wears stylish wire-rimmed glasses. Loves computers. A former lawyer and friend calls him "a geek." This description is backed up by snippets of phone conversations recorded by the FBI in 1999, at the start of the investigation. Mixed in with discussions about the "vig" (the vigorish, or interest) and the "tab" (the principal on a debt), there is Scarfo boasting to another young wiseguy about his new computer.

"I got a monster," he says. "I got a f—ing DVD in there . . . 128 megs of RAM, a Pentium III 450 . . . a 19-inch monitor and Digital Surround Sound. The whole f—ing nine yards."

The kid's first serious brush with the law came in 1989 when he was the victim of a Mob hit. On Halloween night, a guy wearing a mask and carrying a trick-or-treat bag walked into Dante & Luigi's restaurant in South Philadelphia, where Scarfo and a friend had just sat down to dinner. The young mobster was having clams and linguini—his favorite dish, according to a friend—when the masked man walked up to Scarfo's table, pulled a MAC-10 submachine pistol out of his bag, and opened fire. Scarfo was hit eight times. Miraculously, he survived, and two weeks later, he walked out of the hospital. You just can't make this stuff up.

In investigating the shooting—to this date, no one has been charged with the crime—detectives seized a laptop computer Scarfo was carrying with him that night. On it, they found gambling and loan-sharking records. Back then, Scarfo wasn't into encryption.

Scarfo hid out in North Jersey after the hit, which most believed was orchestrated by a renegade faction of the Philadelphia Mob upset with the reign of his father. Since the elder Scarfo was in jail at the time, his son became a proxy target.

A year later, young Nicky was popped by the New Jersey State Police on charges involving the sale and distribution of illegal videopoker machines. Scarfo eventually pleaded guilty and served about three and a half years. In 1997, while still on parole, he got involved in a barroom fight in Atlantic City. He again pleaded guilty, this time to a weapons charge, and was sentenced to another 18 months.

Along the way, Scarfo also managed to spend time in the Clearwater, Florida, area working for a computer software company owned by a friend. The company's name was America's Most Wanted Software. The kid has always had a sense of humor.

The Investigation Gets Under Way

It was back in North Jersey in 1998, after his release from prison on the weapons charge, that Scarfo showed up again on the FBI's radar screen. A Gambino crime-family associate who was about to go to jail needed someone to oversee his bookmaking and loan-sharking operation. Scarfo, the feds say, was tapped to handle the job.

In December 1998, the FBI began tracking Scarfo. The first search warrant was issued on January 15, 1999. The feds seized data from one of the computers in his business office in Belleville, a small town adjacent to Newark. They also grabbed three wads of cash from the young mobster, which was not surprising. January 15 was a Friday. Friday is the day when bookies settle up with their bettors.

Scarfo had $6,011 in cash in his pockets that day. The money was separated into three bundles, each wrapped with rubber bands. He also was carrying what investigators identified as a "computer generated printout" of gambling and loansharking records.

The FBI took the contents of the hard drive from Scarfo's computer and transferred it to a disk. During a later analysis, investigators discovered that one document, labeled "Factors," had been encrypted in a program known as PGP—Pretty Good Privacy. Available in most software outlets, the 128-bit PGP encryption program is considered one of the best on the market and is virtually impossible to crack.

"Factors" had last been modified on January 12, a Tuesday.

According to an FBI affidavit that is part of the investigative file, Tuesday is the usual day for finalizing wins and losses in an illegal gambling operation. "Attempts to decrypt this file without the pass phrase were unsuccessful," the affidavit notes.

[Scarfo] was carrying what investigators identified as a 'computer generated printout' of gambling and loansharking records.

Stymied, federal authorities went back to court and asked for a search warrant that authorized another break-in to Scarfo's office. In May, the FBI's black-bag operatives hit the business and planted the keystroke recorder. While the specifics remain under wraps, the prevailing theory is that a tiny, battery-powered device was secreted in the keyboard of Scarfo's computer. The recorder then sent a signal to an FBI surveillance post—perhaps a van not far from Scarfo's office—from which the feds could monitor the activity occurring on Scarfo's terminal.

The court order approved monitoring for about 60 days. In fact, authorities now say, they were "up" on the keystroke recorder for only 14 days. In the end, the feds found the pass phrase that gave them access to what prosecutors now claim are gambling and loan-sharking records. Those records are the heart of the case against Nicodemo S. Scarfo.

Privacy Violations?

A year later, on June 21, 2000, a grand jury handed up a three-count indictment charging Scarfo and an associate with gambling and loan-sharking. But the trial has been on hold while lawyers argue over privacy rights, the Constitution, and what critics contend is an egregious example of 21st-century Big Brotherism. The issue, says Sobel of the Electronic Privacy Information Center (EPIC), is "how a Fourth Amendment search should be conducted in an electronic environment." The fact that it is a Mob book making case, he adds, is immaterial.

In their legal briefs, Scarfo's attorneys claim they need to know how the keystroke recorder works in order to fashion a motion seeking to have the evidence thrown out. The attorneys believe that investigators did not have the proper court authorization to secretly monitor Scarfo's computer activities. At the very least, his lawyers say, the FBI should have sought a more difficult-to-obtain wiretap authorization.

Wiretap laws require that the authorities stop listening when what is being said is not relevant to the criminal investigation. For example, if a bug is placed on a target's phone and the target calls his doctor rather than his partner in crime, those listening in are required to shut down their listening device. The conversation with the doctor is private. And it is protected. In contrast, sifting through a hailstorm of keystrokes—including, presumably, personal correspondence—to find a computer password doesn't allow for that kind of selective snooping. In fact, the defense claims, the investigation was a blatant and illegal invasion of Scarfo's privacy.

In court filings, the government has insisted that it did not intercept any electronic communications from Scarfo's computer to the outside world and that therefore it was not necessary to obtain wiretap authorization. Furthermore, the FBI maintains that the recorder was specifically set to "capture the pass phrase and key-related information." But without a more detailed explanation, defense attorneys remain skeptical.

[Scarfo's] lawyers say [that] the FBI should have sought a more difficult-to-obtain wiretap authorization.

Following a hearing in August [2001], Scarfo's lawyers joked about how the feds had overreached in the case, employing the high-tech surveillance that should have been used to track terrorists and other threats to national security to build a case against the son of a jailed Mafia don, a son who happened to be more computer-literate than your typical wiseguy, but who was a low level wiseguy nonetheless.

"It's hard to believe the government would risk national security on a gambling case," said Vincent Scoca, one of the defense lawyers, who compared the investigation to domestic spying. "These are the same techniques used to hunt down terrorists," he added.

Norris Gelman, another Scarfo lawyer, then weighed in with his comment about Osama bin Laden betting on the Detroit Lions. At the time, his sardonic, off-the-cuff comment seemed to capture the David-and-Goliath and Big-Brother-Is-Watching elements of the case.

But after the attacks of September 11, no one was laughing.

Post–September 11 Law Enforcement

In the initial hearings about the keystroke recorder, Judge Nicholas Politan expressed skepticism about the government's less-than-forthright explanations of the technology. Three times he referred to the high-tech jargon that was spread throughout the government's motions as "gobbledygook." But two weeks after the attacks on the World Trade Center towers and the Pentagon, prosecutors met with Politan in a private, *ex parte* hearing and provided the judge with classified information about the device. Following the hearing, Politan ruled that the government did not have to give defense lawyers a detailed description of the keystroke recorder. Instead, the judge said, a nonclassified summary description would suffice.

Even Gelman, a leading defense attorney in the Philadelphia area, concedes that these are trying times and that, in special circumstances, some individual rights may have to be sacrificed. "I have absolutely no compunction, if you are looking to stop a bombing or some other form of terrorist attack, to calibrating the rights of privacy in regard to the gravity of the offense," he said. "If someone is planning to strap on a bomb and blow himself and others up or if someone is planning to fly a plane into a building, then privacy rights may not be the paramount concern."

"But bookmaking would not be in that category of offenses."

So while many people—probably many more now than before September 11—may concede the need for more government secrecy and greater investigative access to certain files and records, a fundamental issue raised in the Scarfo case remains unanswered. How and when should that secrecy and access be permitted? The sweeping new electronic surveillance powers that were signed into law in October [2001]—broader use of wiretaps and the expanded ability to track emails, for example, further underscore the concerns raised in the Scarfo case. Among other things, the case shows that the potential for abuse and misuse of those powers was high even before September 11.

With more and more people storing their personal, private, and business records on computers, Sobel, the general counsel for EPIC, says there is a need for legislation to deftly define what the government can and cannot do in this new, ever-changing electronic age. At this point, Sobel says, technology has outpaced existing law. Neither the framers of the Constitution, with its Fourth Amendment privacy-rights protection, nor the authors of the Tire III wiretap laws, which have long governed how and when Big Brother can listen, envisioned the sophisticated electronic world in which we now live, work, and communicate.

A fundamental issue raised in the Scarfo case remains unanswered. How and when should [government] secrecy and access be permitted?

Alan Hart, who heads the Department of Criminal Justice at Burlington County College in New Jersey, said the issues raised in the Scarfo case are Orwellian. "This doesn't 'smack' of Big Brotherism," he said. "It hits you over the head like a baseball bat."

Joking Until the End

Young Nicky Scarfo has politely but firmly declined to discuss his case. "Talk to my lawyer," he told reporters following one hearing in Newark late last summer [2001]. "It's all in their [motions]. You got more than enough to write about."

Then he went on to tell a story about his new wife and a problem with a mouse in their apartment. His wife wanted him to use "humane" traps to capture the rodent, he said. For days, no luck. "It was a smart mouse," he said.

But the mouse went too far. Thought he had the run of the place. One night he munched his way through a bag of Doritos, one of Mrs. Scarfo's favorite snack foods.

The next day, standard mousetraps baited with peanut butter and cheese were in place. A short time later, the mouse problem was solved.

Scarfo laughed. He wasn't a violent person, he said, but then, borrowing a phrase that came up a lot during his father's day, he noted that sometimes "you gotta do what you gotta do."

The kid has always had a sense of humor. Consider the pass phrase he was using for his encrypted files. When the feds got the keystroke recorder up and running, they were finally able to identify it: nds09813-050.

Nds09813-050 is the coded federal prison identification for the kid's father, Nicodemo D. "Little Nicky" Scarfo.

7

Mobsters' Sons Are Becoming Suburban Hoods

Mike McAlary

The late New York Daily News columnist Mike McAlary won the Pulitzer Prize for his journalistic commentary in 1998, the year he died of cancer. He regularly covered the New York crime beat, tackling stories about the mob and police corruption. He also put his knowledge of crime and scandal to use in writing best-selling fiction such as Buddy Boys; Cop Shot; Good Cop, Bad Cop; *and the book-form treatment of the film* Copland.

The sons of New York's Mafia gangsters are the products of two worlds. They grew up in a life of privilege outside of Mafia dealings and thus have more in common with suburban "mall rats" than with hoods who prowl city streets. However, their recognition that they are the scions of Mafiosi has led them to venerate that lifestyle and embrace crime and violence. The mixed breeding has produced "wannabe" gangsters who are nonetheless dangerous. Darin Mazzarella was one such Mafia youth who— seduced by media images of the Mafia and entranced by the book deals that await incarcerated mobsters—formed a gang of like-minded punks and graduated from petty theft and fistfights up to armed robbery and murder. Eventually, Mazzarella was caught, but like many mobsters, he turned informant to escape imprisonment. Mazzarella is one of many Mafia sons who lack the integrity that supposedly goes along with a mob pedigree and view crime and violence as simply part of the romance of the gangster life.

The young mobster, who carried himself more like [football player] Brett Favre than like John Gotti, was wearing a wool J. Crew sweater and a green rain slicker against the sweeping winter wind. As he stepped off the U.S.S. *Nautilus*, the nuclear submarine docked in Groton, Connecticut, the low sky was gray and cold. This aging monument to a world below the surface, I thought, was the perfect place to meet the latest gangster turned rat.

To see the new face of the mob, look no further than 27-year-old Darin Mazzarella. He is slope-shouldered, about five feet ten and 180 pounds, with reddish hair. Like a retired quarterback with ruined knees, he has horrific scars and a severe limp—the legacy of an incident two summers ago, when he took fourteen bullets from a mob rival outside a crowded Bronx playground. Instead of wearing sharkskin suits and listening to Frank Sinatra, the new young mobsters favor Eddie Bauer jeans and Annie Lennox CD's while committing their mayhem. The Goodfellas days of Henry Hill and the Robert's Lounge in South Ozone Park, Queens, are long gone. Until last year [1997], Darin Mazzarella, along with the sons of gangsters who were his lifelong buddies, hung out not in social clubs in Little Italy and on Staten Island but at a low-rent strip shopping center in Yonkers. They're suburban rats.

When I meet him for the first time in Groton, he is still jail-pale after being held for eight months without bail in the 1994 murder of a Westchester politician's kid. Mazzarella and his vicious brother, Nicholas, had been in protective custody for a month. The FBI had sprung Darin from a county jail cell, ostensibly to marry his high-school sweetheart, and then made it look like the suspected killer was under house arrest so he could wear a wire around his pals.

A former high-school baseball star and community-college engineering student, Darin Mazzarella is a keen but barbed character who talks philosophically about the future of "the gangster soul." Like John Gotti Jr., he is where New York's mob story is headed.

Meeting the Mobster

For four years, I had been following Mazzarella and a wanton crew called the Tanglewood Boys who had been terrorizing Yonkers and the Bronx and had recently extended their brutal reach to the Upper West Side of Manhattan. One day last fall, after he became a protected federal informant, Darin called me at home saying he wanted to talk face-to-face. Mazzarella, who is now in the witness-protection program along with his brother and their wives, suggested we meet at the submarine base.

"I was gonna send you e-mail from a public library near where the FBI has my family stashed, but the computers they got aren't modern enough," Darin explained when we met. "I used one of those phone cards the mob is selling now to call you." We wound up in a Ground Round restaurant, sitting at a wooden table, surrounded by sailors. The Jets were playing the Minnesota Vikings at the Meadowlands, and with the televisions blaring, no one seemed to notice us at first.

"Back when I was locked up, I saw Sammy Gravano[1] talking on television with Diane Sawyer," Mazzarella said. "I was left to twist in the wind by guys who hired high-priced lawyers like Ben Brafman. I was in jail protecting wiseguys who weren't doing s— for me. The guys in my own crew ain't even paying my fiancée money they owe me. Then I see Gravano on television. Here's a boss who ratted, kept his money, wrote a book—and I'm thinking, What the f— am I doing? I'm gonna be the last stand-up guy? F— that. Like politics, the gangster culture has bottomed out. Even the mob bosses we aspire to be have movie deals."

1. the Gambino family mobster who turned informant against John Gotti Sr.

Mazzarella was talking too loudly, and I was concerned that a couple of sailors nearby had him on their radar. The waitress coughed. Darin lowered his voice to a whisper.

"You know, when you were writing about the Tanglewood Boys all the time, I was gonna come down to Manhattan one night and baseball-bat you," he confessed. "You were in one of our clubs, and I got beeped. 'McAlary is in here right now, with his wife.' This was a big going-away party for somebody from your newspaper."

I was jolted into remembering a dark, velvet-covered room.

"Yeah, that's our place," he continued. "The Genovese [family] capo [captain] who used to run hiring at the Javits Center is the secret owner. At the same time the [New York] *Daily News* is screaming about the Javits mob, you're renting our nightclub!"

"We didn't know."

"I didn't come down and whack you because I realized, hey, if I ever get in trouble, you know, maybe I'll need you. We could be partners."

"Partners? In what?"

"You know, partners in a book-and-movie deal."

Darin the Informant

On December 13, 1997, as the federal collar tightened on Junior Gotti and 40 others, including Tanglewood Boys past and present, Darin surfaced again at the submarine base, this time wearing a Tommy Hilfiger shirt. He and his brother had just pleaded guilty to federal racketeering charges in White Plains and agreed to cooperate with prosecutors. Even though news of the arrangement wouldn't get out for nearly two weeks, Darin wanted to tell me about the crimes he had committed between 1989 and 1995 with several generations of established Gambino, Genovese, and Lucchese gangsters.

Before he is sentenced for racketeering, Mazzarella's keepers say, he will testify against his old boss, Anthony "Blue Eyes" Santorelli, in a half-dozen state and federal trials covering a wide variety of crimes, including mob murders, assaults, armed robberies, hijackings, loan-sharking, and ruthless mob extortion schemes involving union jobs and building construction. Although most of his testimony will focus on his involvement with the Lucchese family, some of his best friends were arrested on January 21 [1998] with Junior Gotti, including several charter members of the Tanglewood Boys. Junior was also found, the government charges, with a list of names the prosecutors have called "The Holy Grail." The list included names of two Lucchese mobsters—Joseph Cosentino and Anthony Magana—who executed John Petrucelli, the father of Darin Mazzarella's best friend.

The Tanglewood Shopping Center on Central Park Avenue in Yonkers is a dingy thirteen-store, one-pay-phone, gray-and-maroon backwoods strip mall just across the street from Nathan's Famous restaurant, where the nice kids hang out. I first began receiving letters from a guy in the Tanglewood gang in 1994, after writing about the murder of Louis Balancio, a student at Mercy College. The writer called himself Jack and wrote single-spaced, severely misspelled letters. He seemed to know a great deal about murders, assaults, arson, and bookmaking operations. In 1993, FBI agent Dave Calore and his supervisor came to see me about the letters. It turned out Jack used to write to the FBI but quit them for me. The agents showed me an advertisement they'd placed in the *Daily News*'s classified section trying to communicate with him. I shared Jack's letters with the FBI, about eight of them. Some of Jack's information was good. Some of it was wrong. The identity and motive of the mysterious mob letter-writer was baffling. Jack knew about bookmaking operations being run by Darin Mazzarella, his friend Alfred "Freddy Boy" Santorelli, and their underlings. He gave me a complete list of the gang, which included the Santorellis, the Mazzarellas, the DiSimones, Johnnie Boy Petrucelli, and ten others. The FBI used this information, and the bookmaking phone numbers Jack provided, to make a 1995 raid near Yankee Stadium, arresting Darin Mazzarella.

"Jack made us be more careful," Darin said. "But we figured it was the FBI writing the letters to you anyway. Only after I agreed to cooperate did I realize Jack actually existed."

Beginnings of a Criminal Life

Mazzarella has since helped the FBI identify Jack, who is also being protected. "Jack helped us break up Tanglewood and solve three murders," said Dave Calore. "He was the real deal."

Darin Mazzarella was living the jock life at Roosevelt High School in Yonkers until 1988, his senior year, when he broke his wrist and had to quit the varsity baseball team. He lived with his mother and Nicholas, 29 [in 1998], in the Crestwood Arms Apartments, behind the Dumpsters in the Tanglewood shopping center. He was from a broken family, the son of an electrical engineer with a union job in the city. The Mazzarella brothers used to hang in the mall near the deli, where they carved their names in the redbrick. Darin also had the word TANGLEWOOD tattooed on his calf.

No cops came around then, but today there is a Dunkin' Donuts in the shopping center, and last month I counted ten Yonkers cops stopping by for coffee in one hour. The strip includes a couple of delis, a pizza store, a Laundromat, a dry cleaner, a Chinese restaurant, and some hairdressers. It's working-middle-class—the stickers on the rear windows of the cars parked there read NEW PALTZ, ALBANY STATE, and NEWBURGH.

By 1989, Darin said, he had abandoned the jock life for the gangster life. In quick succession, he'd dropped out of community college, grabbed a mob construction job in Manhattan, and dreamed of becoming a gangster like the ones in the movies he rented from Tanglewood Video. Instead of playing baseball, he began stealing rare baseball cards, selling Mickey Mantle and Henry Aaron rookie cards to Lucchese mobsters for as much as $6,000 each. By then, there were about twenty Tanglewood Boys hanging out in the parking lot, listening to [disc jockeys] Mike and the Mad Dog on WFAN or Hot 97 FM and selling stolen goods, splitting gambling receipts, loan-sharking, or robbing local supermarkets and fast-food stores with guns.

"We were like every mall kid you ever saw in the nineties, only we got the sons of six gangsters in the Tanglewood parking lot almost every night," Darin told me. "We got Anthony DiSimone and Freddy Boy Santorelli from the Lucchese family. Johnnie Boy Petrucelli is the son of a guy who got whacked for hiding a guy who killed a federal agent. Stevie Crea is the son of the Lucchese underboss. There is Craig DePalma, the son of a Gambino capo; Greg DePalma, who is with Junior Gotti. Pasquale Parrello is around, too. He's the son of a Genovese soldier, Patsy Parrello. The kid got whacked after his father slapped Torrie Locascio, the son of Frank Locascio, the Gambino underboss guy who went away with John Gotti. We would hang out there before we went to the clubs, listening to music. We liked everything from Springsteen and Billy Joel to Neil Diamond and even the black gangsta rap. Anything but Metallica. . . .

We were like every mall kid you ever saw in the nineties.

"We used to go to clubs all over Westchester and the Bronx and beat the s— out of people. We were just raging through the night. We intimidated the old wiseguys. We got free drinks, and if we started a fight, the other guys got thrown out. We dressed like clean-cut college kids, and we even used to make fun of gangsters in those stupid white-on-white shirts and silk suits. Our heroes were [New York Giants star] Phil Simms, [New York Yankees player] Don Mattingly, and Mobster John

Gotti. How could you not like the way he dressed? We would do robberies and go shopping at Take Six and Century 21 in Manhattan. Mostly we wore Gap clothes or Nike outfits. We thought we looked better than the old-timers.

"Out of high school, I had a brand-new Cougar, and Freddy Boy had a brand-new maroon iroc Camaro convertible. You sleep till noon. You got girls and cash. You go on vacations whenever you like. Anybody that doesn't like it got to be insane. We played softball and football, and when guys owed me and Freddy money, we took their rice rockets too—red, white, and blue Kawasaki motorcycles. Once, Freddy took this guy's girlfriend. He just called this guy down to Tanglewood and told him, 'If you see her again, I'll break your legs.' Freddy even got engaged to the stolen girl. We didn't give a s— about wiseguys, though we respected them because they were older. They had guns. We had guns. We had fathers to protect us. So we did what the f— we wanted. It's great until you go to jail. Then the betrayal starts."

Robberies and Murder

Darin's first and closest mob friend was Johnnie Boy Petrucelli. Because of his deal with the prosecutor, Darin had to give Petrucelli up in three murders, including the 1995 stabbing of a 17-year-old in the Bronx. In the eighties, he and Johnnie Boy would do gangster sleepovers at Petrucelli's mother's house in Ardsley. They also frequented a New Rochelle restaurant where John Petrucelli Sr., who liked cocaine and silk suits, hung out five nights a week in the back room. John Sr. was a big partyer but a rebel gangster who never wanted to go to Brooklyn to his boss.

Mostly we wore Gap clothes or Nike outfits. We thought we looked better than the old-timers.

For as long as there has been a Mafia its story has been one of fathers and sons. The senior Petrucelli was a convicted

Lucchese hit man who shot two guys in a Bronx bar in the late sixties. He claimed it was an argument over heroin, but it was a classic mob hit. He fled, and the mob, of course, protected him. But eventually he went to trial, and was out on bail waiting across the street from the Bronx Criminal Courthouse when someone relayed the guilty verdict. Petrucelli fled again. After nearly ten years on the lam, he was captured in Florida and shipped to Green Haven. Sometimes Petrucelli's sons—Johnnie Boy and Joey—would travel upstate to see him. The kids were enthralled with the gangster's life and charmed by their father's notion of fealty. It is all romantic fable, but the Petrucelli boys took it for truth.

In prison, Petrucelli befriended a muscular young gangster named Constabile "Gus" Farace. When another inmate threatened to drop a set of weights on Petrucelli's head, Farace saved him. Petrucelli returned the favor after their release from prison. On February 28, 1989, while working on a drug deal, Farace shot and killed Everett Hatcher, a federal undercover agent. The murder was front-page tabloid news for weeks. Farace, now wanted by the Feds and the mob, turned to his Green Haven family, and John Petrucelli, then 47, agreed to hide him. A Lucchese boss sent word to John Petrucelli: "Either clip Farace or kill yourself." He refused, and on September 13, 1989, Petrucelli was executed by his boyhood friend Joey "Blue Eyes" Cosentino and Anthony Magana, two names that would wind up on Junior Gotti's list. In time, their sons went to war, the fight going on in the name of their mob fathers.

The Petrucelli boys and the Cosentino boys began to ricochet through the mob world. On March 8, 1992, outside a New Rochelle bar where Darin worked as a bouncer, the younger Petrucelli son, Joey, 16, got into a racial argument and shot another 16-year-old to death. He is doing a life bit. Johnnie Boy Petrucelli and Darin Mazzarella have beaten up on the Cosentino boys and were planning to kill them when the FBI came crashing down.

"Johnnie Boy definitely wanted to revenge his father," Darin said. "I remember his dad's wake in the Bronx. I was like 18 and didn't know all the wiseguys then. It was mostly Johnnie's friends. The Petrucelli brothers went crazy after that. I started a life of crime with Johnnie Boy. His father was on his way out of a girlfriend's apartment trying to get to his navy-blue Mazda 929 when he got hit. Johnnie Boy got the car when the FBI was done with it. All the panels were ripped out. We didn't care. We still drove it around. That was kind of weird, I guess, driving around in FBI evidence.

The [Petrucelli] kids were enthralled with the gangster's life and charmed by their father's notion of fealty.

"After his father's closed-casket funeral, Johnnie got the car and $4,000 cash from his grandmother, and I stood by Johnnie. We tried to make money and started using the car to do robberies. The FBI crime scene was the getaway car. The first crime we did was rob a New Rochelle bookmaker one night in 1989. We just knocked on his door and Johnnie stuck an unloaded gun in his face. We grabbed $3,500 and left the guy in his bathtub. Then we started robbing baseball cards in Yonkers and Hartsdale and spending money on clothes at the Cross County Mall. Our technique was simple: Break the glass with a baseball bat and run in.

"We robbed assault rifles from a sporting-goods store. We were down in the Bronx when some Albanians we were always arguing with shot up our cars. Johnnie Boy came back and killed one of them outside a bar. That was his first murder.

"Then Johnnie told me he killed another guy to revenge his brother, Joey. Johnnie said he just ran into a crowd of kids in the Bronx and stabbed one kid to death. He didn't even know if it was the right guy and didn't care. I gave the FBI Johnnie's three murders. It will be difficult to testify against him, though. Loyalty died with his old man, but Johnnie never betrayed me."

Arrest

By 1991, Darin Mazzarella had moved from violence to book-making. He opened an office in a building controlled by a friend's father on 109th Street, between First and Second Avenues, and was making $100,000 on some weekends. The crack dealers on the corner never messed with Anthony "Blue Eyes" Santorelli's Tanglewood Boys.

They still gathered in the parking lot, but the Tanglewood Boys were rich now. On February 2, 1992, the Mazzarella brothers went to a friend's house for a party in Tuckahoe. An older Gambino associate was snorting coke in the bathroom all night and teasing Nick Mazzarella, who then grabbed the guy by the throat and choked him. He fell to the floor, unconscious. Another Tanglewood Boy ran into the kitchen and stabbed him in the neck with a kitchen knife.

We started robbing baseball cards in Yonkers and Harts-dale and spending money on clothes at the Cross County Mall.

"I never saw anyone killed before," Darin recalled. "Instead of people breaking the stereo while his parents were away, we killed somebody in this kid's house. We wrapped his body in a handmade quilt, and I drove his van with the body to Manhattan. We had just seen *Goodfellas* and were listening to the CD on the stereo. I left the van on the Upper East Side with a body." The case went unsolved until Darin and Nick, who were both wired by the FBI, ratted out their friends. Nick pleaded guilty to the murder last month, and Darin admitted dumping the body.

Then, on February 4, 1994, the Tanglewood Boys killed a 21-year-old Mercy College student in a very public way. Louis Balancio was knifed to death outside the Strike Zone Bar, a mob hangout, now closed, across the street from Darin's high school in Yonkers. Although there may have been as many as 30 witnesses, none came forward. . . .

Mazzarella was arrested for the murder in December 1996. Jeanine Pirro, the Westchester D.A.; Mary Joe White, the federal prosecutor; and James Kallstrom, the former assistant director of the New York FBI office, announced the arrests. In August 1997, Darin's future wife met with Calore [the FBI agent who helped catch Mazzarella] on the sly and told him that Darin wanted to turn. In February, the D.A. quietly dropped the murder charges against Mazzarella. . . .

Following his release from jail in August [1997], Darin went to work for the FBI. Now he is looking for a partner, someone to write his story. It won't be me.

8

The Mafia Is Recruiting Sicilian Mobsters

Clarence Walker

Clarence Walker is a journalist in Houston, Texas. He has written a few articles on the mob for Rick Porrello's AmericanMafia .com Web site.

Because federal authorities have been so successful in thwarting mob rackets, and because the mob itself has been plagued by turncoats, the American Mafia is actively recruiting new members from Sicily. The Sicilian gangsters are hardened by years of experience in controlling crime on their native island, and, unlike many of their American counterparts, they are expected to have a greater sense of honor and respect for Mafia codes of behavior. Many of these imported thugs have already filled the declining ranks of major crime families in New York, Chicago, and Philadelphia. In addition, many young American mobsters have been sent to Sicily to learn the criminal trade from their more experienced and dedicated kin. Law enforcement is worried that the new blood and the reemphasis on strict allegiance to Mafia codes will reinvigorate the currently lifeless and near-defeated mob in America.

Remember this public service announcement? "The Marines are looking for a few good men." Now, can anyone

Clarence Walker, "American Mafia Recruits Sicilian Mafia," www.AmericanMafia.com, August 2004. Copyright © 2004 by Clarence Walker. Reproduced by permission.

believe this? The American (Italian) mafia is also looking for good men. They are desperate to recruit fresh blood.

Overthrown by mafia turncoats, aggressive law enforcement and (RICO [Racketeer Influenced and Corrupt Organizations Act]) prosecution of mafia brothers across the nation has left the Italian crime families in America decimated in recent years. Famous traitors like informants Sammy "Bull" Gravano, Henry Hill, Ralph Natale, Angelo Lonardo, and the murder and imprisonment of hundreds of Mafiosos have, in fact, galvanized crime families into desperation. As the saying goes, "no honor among thieves". It seems there's no silence and honor among some of America's toughest Mafiosos which has given law enforcement, for years, access to penetrate mafia organizations and flip soldiers to break the mafia silence code and betray their masters and bosses.

"The American mafia is a shell of what it used to be," says Captain Steven O'Donnell of the Rhode Island state police. O'Donnell infiltrated the Patriarca family for six years by posing as an associate. Mafia godfathers may turn in their graves but the American mafia is seeking new talent, preferably of Sicilian origin, to recruit into the crime family organizations. Highly in demand are Mafiosos willing to die than break the "omerta" code of silence, willing to kill enemies, rivals; if necessary, kill American government officials. This is no exaggeration. According to FBI and foreign investigators, the Italian mafia, to find their perception of good men, are reaching across the globe into their homeland of Sicily, Italy, to find honorable men to uphold principles of the "real" mafia. U.S. and Italian organized crime investigators indicated the American mafia is recruiting Sicilian mafia criminals because they now believe their counterparts in Sicily "are more honorable to mafia principles than Italian Mafiosos in America." Sicilian mafia criminals' migration into America has alarmed U.S. authorities. Authorities are highly concerned the Sicilian mafia, known in the past for gunning down police and blowing up judges and prosecutors might bring this kind of handiwork into the American mafia. FBI officials discussed the high-alert topic in Washington, D.C., and New York [in 2004]. . . .

Filling the Ranks

"This type of phenomenon (recruiting in Sicily) was born when American authority's action grew stronger and more effective, which, in recent years reached a crescendo in Chicago, Philadelphia and New York," the chief of Italy's anti-mafia commission, Senator Roberto Centaro, said during interviews in New York with the FBI, DEA [Drug Enforcement Administration], the U.S. Protection for Mafia Informants and the Justice Department. "These are the areas where the families move to recruit in Sicily." Recruitment of Sicilian mafia criminals into the American mafia were exposed over a year ago when a top Sicilian mafia informant revealed the secretive information to Italian and U.S. law enforcement, "that was confirmed by U.S. and Italian wiretaps," said Centaro. Dozens of Sicilians between the ages of twenty and thirty, according to intelligence sources, were sent from towns of the Palermo area to help shore up the ranks of clans in New York, Chicago, and Philadelphia. Using phone taps, U.S. authorities have heard new arrivals discussing attacks on American investigators and judges. The FBI and U.S. Justice Department have declined to confirm or deny the information regarding possible attacks on American government officials. Matthew Heron, Assistant FBI Agent in charge of the organized crime branch in the FBI's New York office, provides insight into the Sicilian recruitment. "A combination of turncoats and convictions," Heron explains, "created 'leadership vacuum' in some crime gangs, particularly the Bonannos and they have reached into Sicily to bring some people over to fill gaps, the rationale being the Sicilians are more inclined to maintain the sacred vow of silence," Heron recently stated in a telephone interview with reporters from New York. "It's not accurate to say they have assumed leadership roles within the family. Yet the fact is they are here, they are establishing themselves. In the foreseeable future, it's safe to say we expect to see them assume leadership." Heron noted the fact the American Italian mafia has always avoided attacking U.S. law enforcement. "From what we've been told, that's not the case with the Sicilians. While authorities try to monitor what tactics the American mafia will make next, they are sending local recruits to Sicilian Island for lessons in thuggery," according to Italy's (ANSA) News agency, which reported details of the interrogation of a Sicilian informant by Italian investigators. The informant provided a goldmine of information. "They (the American mafia) send recruits over to Sicily to make them become honorable men, to train them, because in America there's this attack on the values, there's no respect any more," ANSA News quoted mobster Antonio Giuffre as telling investigators. "The American mafia is different and they need some of our qualities." Giuffre's account was confirmed by chief Palermo prosecutor, Piero Grasso. "Every now and then, they'll send someone whose origins are in these areas so they can do serious Mafia lessons," Grasso stated.

A Close Affiliation

"The Sicilian and American Italian mafia have affected each other reciprocally, according to circumstances," said Professor Salvatore Lupo, a mafia expert at the University of Palermo. "They have a common heritage. From what we know, they're not the same thing." During the 1960s, if not earlier, the Sicilian and Italian mafia were distinct organizations but due to family ties and business interests, they often linked up to score 'dirty' money.

For example: during the 1980s, U.S. and Italian prosecutors discovered a link between the Sicilians and the American mafia involvement in a massive drug ring called "The Pizza Connection." Unlike the Sicilians, the Italian mafia agreed to never kill law enforcement or government officials. Showing no mercy or restraint, the Sicilian mafia of the 1980s and 1990s launched the "massacre strategy", killing anyone brave enough to oppose it. This deadly operation caused the 1992 slayings of two nationally admired prosecutors, Giovanni Falcone and Paolo Borsellino, both killed in bomb blasts. Italians were outraged and a major crackdown followed. As for the new Sicilian recruits migrating onto American soil authorities are keeping close tabs on their activities. "These folks coming over from Sicily are of a different mindset," FBI Agent Heron says. "It's not outside the realm of possibility, and it's something we want to keep a close eye on."

9

The Mafia Has Moved into White-Collar Crime

CNN/Money

CNN/Money is the Internet version of Money magazine, a Time-Warner publication. Like its print counterpart, CNN/Money writers focus on issues related to the U.S. economy, technological trends, and personal finance.

In 2000, law enforcement authorities nabbed 120 people during the bust of a securities fraud scheme in New York City. The perpetrators were selling bogus stocks in the low-price securities market to unsuspecting victims. Eleven of those charged with the crime were alleged members of the Mafia, illustrating that the mob has progressed in recent years from bookmaking and extortion to committing white-collar crimes. The case also revealed that the Internet has become a tool of the mob because most of the advertisements for the fictitious stock deals were sent out via e-mail. This trend in embracing computer-age technology and using it to commit crime is relatively new to Mafia rackets, yet it exemplifies how the Mafia remains a powerful criminal force in America.

In what authorities are calling the largest securities-fraud bust in U.S. history, 120 defendants—including members of all five New York City Mafia crime families and the treasurer of New York City's police-detectives pension fund—were in-

CNN/Money, "Feds Nab 120 for Fraud," http://money.cnn.com, June 14, 2000. Copyright © 2000 by Cable News Network, Inc. Reproduced by permission.

dicted Wednesday [June 14, 2000] for allegedly participating in a securities-fraud scheme involving racketeering and physical violence and costing investors $50 million.

FBI and SEC [Securities Exchange Commission] officials said this case represents an emerging trend of the New York crime families banding together to infiltrate the securities markets. However, they pointed out that they have not infiltrated the mainstream securities markets, but a small portion of the low-price securities, or "micro-cap," market.

The result of a 10-month investigation called Operation Uptick were sixteen indictments and seven criminal complaints, issued in connection with the publicly traded securities of 19 companies and the private placement of securities of 16 companies over five years, including the fast-food chain Ranch 1.

Among those indicted were: 11 alleged members and associates of organized crime; 57 licensed and unlicensed stockbrokers; three recruiters of corrupt brokers; 12 stock promoters; 30 officers, directors or other "insiders" of the companies issuing the securities; two accountants; an attorney; an investment adviser and a hedge fund manager. Defendants could face jail terms ranging from five to 80 years.

The List of Crimes

Mary Jo White, [former] U.S. attorney for the Southern District of New York, Barry Mawn, assistant director [now retired] of the New York office of the FBI, and Richard Walker, [former] director of enforcement for the U.S. Securities & Exchange Commission, announced the indictments at a press conference in lower Manhattan Wednesday.

"This is the largest securities fraud takedown in history," said White.

Charges included racketeering, securities fraud, pension fund fraud, bribery of brokers and union officials, extortion, money laundering, witness tampering and solicitation to commit murder in nationwide security schemes worth more than $50 million, White said. The methods used, she said, included "controlling crews of corrupt brokers, sometimes entire branches of brokerage firms, bribing other brokers to sell and fraudulently inflate the price of stocks, running high-pressure boiler rooms, bribing union officials and fiduciaries to breach their duty to their members, and using violence and threats of violence to enforce and tighten the enterprise's criminal grip."

The enterprise was "enhanced by the use and abuse of the Internet," White said, alleging that e-mail blitzes were sent to prospects—often senior citizens—"to fraudulently hype stocks."

Early Wednesday morning, 600 FBI agents and police officers arrested 98 of the 120 defendants in New York, New Jersey, Connecticut, Pennsylvania, Maryland, Virginia, Georgia, Florida, Alabama, Texas, Illinois, Utah and California.

This was the largest number of people ever arrested at one time on securities-fraud-related charges, and one of the largest number ever arrested in a criminal case of any kind. White said more arrests were expected. The defendants were all being arraigned in Federal court in Manhattan Wednesday.

Fraudulent Stock and Fictitious Corporations

The charges involve schemes in which members of a central brokerage center called DMN Capital Investments Inc.—operated by men with links to the Bonanno and Colombo crime families, namely Salvatore Piazza, 48, of Howard Beach, N.Y., and James S. Labate, 45, of Staten Island—allegedly infiltrated licensed broker/dealers, bribing them to sell penny stocks, some of which were for dummy companies, to unsuspecting investors, many of whom were senior citizens.

DMN Capital was "fraud central," White said. "It was truly an investment bank to the crooked and the corrupt."

Since last December [1999], the FBI has secretly bugged the company's offices, she said, recording more than 1,000 hours of conversation that led officials to conclude, "The degree and reach of this racketeering enterprise knew no bounds."

One of the companies in which investors were allegedly duped into investing was called Wamex Holdings Inc., which had a market capitalization of $184 million and was supposedly set to initiate a new alternative stock-trading system on July 4 [2000], SEC officials said. The company—of which little financial information is available—went so far as to put a banner advertisement on the Yahoo! Web portal this morning [Wednesday, June 14] and had planned to initiate a television-ad campaign, officials said.

The degree and reach of this racketeering enterprise knew no bounds.

"The company never engaged in any illegal activity and it has no relationship with the mob," said Sascha Mundstein, who identified himself as Wamex's chief operating officer. The defendants were also indicted for allegedly making illegal private placements of shares of the Ranch 1 fast-food chain and companies called Manhattan Soup Man and Jackpot Entertainment.

Two officers of the Ranch 1 chain, Sebastian Rametta and James F. Chickara, are among those charged with racketeering and are alleged associates of the Colombo crime family.

One of the defendants, Allen Wolfson, a Salt Lake City, Utah securities dealer, allegedly bribed brokers to promote the shares of such small cap companies as Beautymerchant.com, Learner's World Inc., Rollerball International Inc., Healthwatch Inc. and HYTK Industries Inc. Wolfson and his associates received at least $7 million in profits from that scheme.

According to the SEC, DMN Capital, the New York–based brokerage house, also acquired majority shares of four companies—Spaceplex Amusement Centers, Reclaim Inc., Beachport Entertainment Group Inc. and International Nursing Services Inc.—and then bribed securities brokers to illegally push shares of those companies to consumers. The brokers got about $3 million in bribes for their participation in the scheme, according to the agency. The principals of DMN, Salvatore Piazza and James Labate, allegedly netted $5 million in profit from the scheme.

Another fraudulent company in which investors were duped into investing was a software company called E-Pawn, with a market capitalization of $198 million. That company had an interest in a smaller Brooklyn company called Learner's World Inc., an alleged Brooklyn day-care center, which had planned to go public in 1999. Authorities say that organized crime netted $3.5 million from the initial 2,000 shares in Learner's World that were to be issued.

Officials suspended trading in Wamex and E-Pawn Wednesday morning "based on inaccurate or incomplete information about those companies presently in the marketplace," said Richard Walker of the Securities and Exchange Commission.

Threats of Violence

Several of the defendants were also charged with threats of physical violence and murder against licensed stockbrokers to force their participation in the schemes. Some stockbrokers were allegedly beaten up for not cooperating.

Another part of the indictment included Stephen E. Gardell, a retired New York City police detective, who, as treasurer of the New York City Detectives' Endowment Association, allegedly took kickbacks from Piazza and Labate to make illegal investments on behalf of the detective's pension fund. Money from this scheme was funneled into offshore accounts and eventually made its way back to the Bonanno crime family, officials said.

In that scheme, corrupt securities industry professionals were allegedly put in charge of managing the detective unions' pension funds, who in turn structured the investments to divert a portion of the funds to the defendants, authorities said.

Frank A. "Frankie" Persico, the alleged Colombo crime family associate, was treasurer of Production Workers Local 400, another union targeted by the racketeering scheme, officials said.

Some stockbrokers were allegedly beaten up for not cooperating [in the scheme].

Gardell, the retired detective, also allegedly leaked confidential law enforcement information about organized crime, helped obtain gun permits for organized crime figures, and influenced the outcome of a New York Police Department investigation into the activities of one of the defendants.

Gardell also allegedly secured parking permits for organized crime members, the complaint said.

Other prominent figures indicted in these schemes include Colombo crime family associates Frank A. Persico and Anthony Stropoli, and Bonanno crime family associate Robert Lino.

Some of the 21 broker dealers and financial firms allegedly infiltrated include Monitor Investment Group Inc., Meyers Pollock and Robbins, First Liberty Investment Group Inc., William Scott & Co., Atlantic General Financial Group, First Fidelity Co., and Bryn Mawr Investment Co.

Officials said plans are in the works to repay some of the investors who were bilked out of their money and that the integrity of the New York City detective's pension fund was not affected.

Though the alleged use of the Internet is a recent development among criminals, Assistant FBI Director Barry Mawn said, many of the practices were familiar: "No matter what market the mob tries to infiltrate, from the fish market to the stock market, their methods are always the same: violence and the threat of violence."

10

The Mafia Is Still a Force in Pop Culture

George De Stefano

George De Stefano is a writer and political activist. His articles focus on Italian American and gay rights issues and have been published in a variety of periodicals, including the Nation *and the* Advocate.

The power of the Mafia is definitely on the decline in America, but the vast amount of mob coverage in the news and in media entertainment would lead one to think otherwise. Television shows such as The Sopranos *and movies such as* Analyze This *propagate Mafia images, leading viewers to assume that mobsters are still a formidable force in America. Worse, however, these movies and television shows often romanticize the mob and play upon Italian American stereotypes to give flavor to stories of death, honor, and a faded way of life. The majority of Italian Americans want to disassociate themselves from the media-created images of the Mafia because surveys have indicated that many Americans have been seduced by these images and assume that anyone of Italian descent must be related to the criminal underworld. The negative stereotypes are such an enduring facet of pop culture that in the public imagination they have eclipsed all the positive contributions made by Italian Americans in the United States.*

George De Stefano, "Ungood Fellas," *Nation,* February 7, 2000. Copyright © 2000 by The Nation Magazine/The Nation Company, Inc. Reproduced by permission.

The last decade of the twentieth century was not a happy one for the Mafia. During the nineties both the United States and Italy made remarkable strides in curbing organized crime, imprisoning gangsters and dismantling their business interests. Though it would be premature to declare either the Italian or the American Mafia dead, both have been wounded, the latter perhaps mortally. But if the Mafia is a shadow of its former self, you'd hardly know it from pop culture. In fact, media images of La Cosa Nostra [the FBI name for the Mafia] seem to be proliferating in direct proportion to the decline of organized crime. Not since Francis Ford Coppola's *The Godfather* reinvented the gangster genre in the early seventies have there been so many wiseguys on screen. The past year brought the films *Analyze This* and *Mickey Blue Eyes,* and with i fratelli [the brothers] Weinstein, Harvey and Bob [the CEOs of Miramax Films], having acquired the rights to the late Mario Puzo's final novel, *Omerta,* for their Miramax Films, there's at least one other high-profile Mafia movie on the way. Another may well be the fourth installment of Coppola's *Godfather* saga. According to the *Hollywood Reporter,* Leonardo Di Caprio and Andy Garcia (Al Pacino's nephew in *Godfather III*) are keen to sign on to the project, pending a suitable script.

On television, gangsters with Italian surnames have been a surefire audience draw, from the days of *The Untouchables* to contemporary cop shows like *NYPD Blue.* A very partial list of recent programs includes the network miniseries *The Last Don* and *Bella Mafia,* as well as biopics about John Gotti and his turncoat lieutenant Sammy "The Bull" Gravano, and, on Showtime cable, an absurdly hagiographic [saintly] one about Joseph Bonanno produced by his son, Bill. But no mob-themed show has generated the critical accolades and viewer enthusiasm accorded *The Sopranos,* the Emmy Award–winning HBO comedy-drama that has become the cable network's most-watched series. . . .

Moving from *The Sopranos'* suburban New Jersey turf to Palermo, HBO last fall [1999] premiered *Excellent Cadavers,* a feature-film adaptation of Alexander Stille's 1995 book about the anti-Mafia campaign launched by two courageous Sicilian magistrates. Why is Italian-American (and Italian) organized crime such a mainstay of American pop culture, and do these images reflect the reality of the Mafia? And does the persistence of the Mafioso as a pop-culture archetype constitute ethnic defamation of Italian-Americans?

Mafia on the Decline in America, but Not in Italy

That many of today's depictions of the American Mafia are in the comic mode—*The Sopranos, Analyze This, Mickey Blue Eyes,* the parody *Mafia!*—is possible only because organized crime is much less fearsome than in its heyday. Both *The Sopranos* and *Analyze This* feature Mafiosi on the verge of a nervous breakdown, their psychological crackups reflecting the disarray of their criminal enterprises under the pressure of law enforcement and the breaking of omerta, the code of silence, by gangsters who'd rather sing than serve time. V. Zucconi, a commentator for the Italian newspaper *La Repubblica,* analyzed this development in an article titled "America: The Decline of the Godfather." Zucconi claims that in the United States the Mafia survives mainly in its pop-culture representations, and that while it used to generate fear, today it is a source of humor. He says that in America one can observe "the funeral of the dying Mafia," an outcome he hopes one day will occur also in Italy. Is Zucconi overoptimistic?

Criminologist James Jacobs reaches a similar conclusion in his study *Gotham Unbound: How New York City Was Liberated from the Clutches of Cosa Nostra* (NYU Press). Organized-crime-control strategies "have achieved significant success in purging Cosa Nostra from the city's social, economic, and political life," he writes. Gangsters in New York, and also in other large and small cities, are losing their foothold in the labor and industrial rackets that have been the source of their power and influence; and there is a dearth of younger, rising stars to replace aging or incarcerated leaders. The decline, says Jacobs, has been so marked that "Cosa Nostra's survival into the next millennium . . . can be seriously doubted." It's a different story in Italy. The Sicilian Mafia's economic might, its alliances with politicians and indifferent law enforcement enabled it to grow so powerful that it threatened Italy's status as a modern nation. As Alexander Stille observed in *Excellent Cadavers,* the war against the Mafia in Sicily is not a local problem of law and order but the struggle for national unity and democracy in Italy. HBO's film based on Stille's book promised to tell that story, but, at barely ninety minutes, it ended up too compressed to offer more than a skim on the events he reported and analyzed so compellingly. . . .

On television, gangsters with Italian surnames have been a surefire audience draw.

In the eighties, Mafia killings accelerated as ambitious upstarts from Corleone (a real place, *Godfather* fans) challenged the Palermo old guard for the control of organized crime. The count included not only Mafiosi but also police officials, magistrates and politicians, who came to be called, with fine Sicilian mordancy, excellent cadavers. Two magistrates, Giovanni Falcone and Paolo Borsellino, began to pursue the Mafia with unprecedented persistence. Their efforts culminated in the historic "maxi-trials," which resulted in the imprisonment of hundreds of Sicily's most powerful gangsters.

The Mafia, of course, retaliated, assassinating Falcone in May 1992 and, two months later, Borsellino. The murders, however, ignited the simmering rage of Sicilians against the Mafia and the officials who protected it. The government was forced to respond, and the subsequent crackdown resulted in the arrest of numerous Mafiosi and connected businessmen and politicians.

Italians overwhelmingly regard Mafiosi as the other; they do not identify or empathize with criminals, nor do they feel that portrayals of organized crime in movies, television and other media tar them with the brush of criminality. Many Italian-Americans, however, regard the seemingly endless stream of Mafia movies and TV shows as a defamatory assault. In mid-January [2000] a coalition of seven Italian-American organizations issued a joint statement condemning *The Sopranos* for "defaming and assassinating the cultural character" of Americans of Italian descent.

Italian-American Stereotypes

It's undeniable that the dominant pop-culture images of Italian-Americans have been the mobster and the related, anti-working class stereotype of the boorish gavone. But there are important differences between these skewed portrayals and other forms of ethnic stereotyping. If the Mafia has been conflated with Sicilian/Italian culture, it's in large part because Italian-American filmmakers and writers have so expertly blended the two. Coppola's memorable and authentic depiction of an Italian-American wedding in *The Godfather* comes to mind. *The Sopranos,* created by veteran TV writer David Chase (nee De Cesare), similarly gets many details right about nouveau riche suburban Italian-Americans, the eponymous mob family's noncriminal neighbors.

The Sopranos cleverly acknowledges Italian-American indignation over Mafia stereotyping only to try to co-opt it. In an episode from the show's first season, Dr. Jennifer Melfi, Tony Soprano's psychiatrist, and her family have a lively dinnertime debate about the persistence of the mob image. The scene ends with the Melfis toasting the "20 million Italian Americans" who have nothing to do with organized crime.

But Jennifer also mocks her ex-husband, an ethnic activist, for being more concerned about "rehabilitating Connie Francis's reputation" than with ethnic cleansing. The line neatly skewers the tunnel vision of conservative Italian-Americans who ignore forms of bias and social injustice that don't affect them. But it also poses a false dichotomy: caring passionately about the image of one's group need not preclude a broader perspective. At other times, the show suggests that Tony, a murderous criminal, is an Italian-American everyman. He's aware of his people's history—he informs his daughter that the telephone was invented not by Alexander Graham Bell but by Antonio Meucci—and he's depicted as more honest and vital than his snooty neighbors, or, as he calls them, the "Wonder-Bread wops."

Sympathetic Pop Culture Icons

The Mafia has become the paradigmatic pop-culture expression of Italian-American ethnicity for several reasons: the aura of glamour, sometimes tragic, surrounding the movie mobster, exemplified by Coppola's Corleones; the gangster genre's embodiment of the violent half of "kiss kiss, bang bang," [film critic] Pauline Kael's famous distillation of the essential preoccupations of American movies; and, perhaps most important, the enduring appeal of the outlaw—the guy who, in a technocratic, impersonal society, has the personal power to reward friends, and, more important, whack enemies. Although real Mafiosi are venal and violent, films and TV too often have presented them far more sympathetically than they deserve— *The Sopranos* is just the latest case in point.

Italian-Americans, whose forebears fled la miseria, the crushing poverty of Southern Italy and Sicily, in numbers so vast that their departure has been likened to a hemorrhage, constitute one of the United States' largest ethnic groups. An Italian-American film critic and author told me some years ago that it was "selfish" of our paesani to complain about Mafia stereotyping given their largely successful pursuit of the American Dream and the more onerous discrimination faced by other minorities. He also insisted that most Americans are smart enough to realize that gangsters constitute only a tiny minority of the Italian-American population.

But it is dismaying—no, infuriating—to see one's group depicted so consistently in such distorted fashion. Unlike racist stereotyping of blacks, portrayals of Italian-American criminality don't reflect or reinforce Italian-American exclusion from American society and its opportunities. (Faced with a threatened NAACP [National Association for the Advancement of Colored People] boycott, both the NBC and ABC networks recently agreed to increase the hiring of blacks, Latinos and Asians, in front of and behind the TV cameras.) The pervasiveness of these images, however, does affect the perception of Italian-Americans by others. Surveys indicate that many Americans believe that most Italian-Americans are in some way "connected" and that Italian immigrants created organized crime in the United States, even though the Irish, Germans and others got there first.

Working to Undo the Negative Images

Besides fostering such attitudes, the Mafia mystique also serves to obscure other, more interesting and no less dramatic aspects of the Italian-American experience. In 1997 the City University of New York hosted a conference on "The Lost World of Italian American Radicalism." Scholars discussed the immigrant anarchists Sacco and Vanzetti (executed by the US government), other major figures like the labor organizer Carlo Tresca, the New York City Congressman Vito Marcantonio and such icons of sixties activism as civil rights advocate Father James Groppi and Mario Savio of the Berkeley Free Speech movement. The conference also highlighted unsung men and women who were labor militants, anti-Fascist organizers and politically engaged writers and artists.

Besides such efforts to recover and understand the radical past, there has been a surge of cultural production and activism among Italian-Americans. In recent years the American-Italian Historical Association, a national organization of academics and grassroots scholars, has held conferences on such hot-button topics as multiculturalism and race relations. Fieri, an association of young Italian-American professionals, [in 1999] commemorated the life and work of Vito Marcantonio, an amazing choice given the far less controversial figures they could have honored. The New York–based Italian-American Writers Association and journals such as Voices in Italian Americana (VIA) and The Italian American Review promote and publish fiction, poetry and critical essays by writers whose vision of italianita flouts the pop-culture cliches. Italo-American gays and lesbians have come out with *Hey, Paisan!*, a new anthology, and *Fuori!*, a folio of essays published by VIA. Actor/playwright Frank Ingrasciotta's *Blood Type: Ragu*, currently enjoying a successful run at the Belmont Italian American Theater in the Bronx (several of whose productions have moved to Off Broadway), offers an exploration of Sicilian-American identity and culture free of goombahs with guns.

The pervasiveness of [Mafia] images . . . does affect the perception of Italian-Americans by others.

Ethnicity remains a powerful and contentious force in American life, and popular culture should illumine its workings. Italian-Americans who want to promote more diverse depictions might not only protest Hollywood film studios and TV production companies. They might put some of the onus on Italian-American creative talents who have built careers on the Mafia. And they could also support the alternative, community-level work being done. Other stories from Italo-America can and should be told.

Organizations to Contact

Central Intelligence Agency (CIA)
Office of Public Affairs, Washington, DC20505
(703) 482-0623 • fax: (703) 482-1739
Web site: www.cia.gov

The CIA assists the president, the National Security Council, and all others who make and execute U.S. national security policy. It provides foreign intelligence regarding national security and conducts counterintelligence activities related to foreign intelligence and national security as directed by the president. The CIA assists U.S. efforts to keep track of foreign criminal organizations such as the Russian Mafia as well as monitoring and combating drug trafficking through such criminal groups. The CIA Web site has some government documents relating to foreign Mafia activities.

Chicago Crime Commission (CCC)
79 W. Monroe, Suite 605, Chicago, IL60603
(312) 372-0101 • fax: (312) 372-6286
e-mail: info@chicagocrimecommission.org
Web site: www.chicagocrimecommission.org

The CCC is a nongovernmental organization that educates the public on current crime issues, implements programs and services that address significant crime problems, reviews and reports on pertinent legislation, and monitors the integrity of law enforcement and criminal justice systems. Its publications include an annual report and a quarterly *Action Alert* newsletter.

Drug Enforcement Administration (DEA)
Mailstop: AXS, 2401 Jefferson Davis Hwy.,
  Alexandria, VA22301
Web site: www.usdoj.gov/dea

The DEA works to enforce the controlled substances laws and regulations of the United States. Its goal is to bring any organization involved in the illegal growing, manufacture, or distribution of controlled substances to the criminal and civil justice system. The DEA is responsible for the development of overall federal drug enforcement strategy, programs, planning, and evaluation. It publishes congressional testimony, press releases, and intelligence reports on the drug trade.

Federal Bureau of Investigation (FBI)
935 Pennsylvania Ave. NW, Room 7350,
  Washington, DC   20535
(202) 324-3000
Web site: www.fbi.gov

The FBI is the principal investigative arm of the U.S. Department of Justice charged with investigating specific crimes against the United States. The FBI has investigative jurisdiction over violations of more than two hundred categories of federal crimes. Top priority has been given to five areas: counterterrorism, organized crime/drugs, foreign intelligence, violent crimes, and financial crimes. The FBI Web site contains an entire section on La Cosa Nostra and its involvement in various criminal activities, including sports betting and labor racketeering.

International Association for the Study of Organized Crime (IASOC)
e-mail: iasoc_office@yahoo.com • Web site: www.iasoc.net

The IASOC is a professional association of educators and researchers covering areas of organized crime. The IASOC publishes a quarterly newsletter entitled *Trends in Organized Crime,* which is available to members, as well as books and articles written by members. The organization's Web site has updated news on the Mafia and other criminal groups.

International Association of Chiefs of Police (IACP)
515 N. Washington St.,
  Alexandria, VA   22314
(703) 836-6767 • fax: (703) 836-4543

e-mail: martinm@theiacp.org (specific to organized crime)
Web site: www.theiacp.org

The association's goals are to advance the science and art of police services. IACP helped create the FBI Identification Division and the Uniform Crime Records system and also spearheaded the national use of fingerprint identification. It publishes *Police Chief* magazine as well as various reports on law enforcement policies, policing trends, and legislative issues.

National Criminal Justice Reference Service
PO Box 6000,
    Rockville, MD 20849-6000
(800) 851-3420
Web site: www.ncjrs.org

A program of the National Institute of Justice, the National Criminal Justice Reference Service serves as a clearinghouse for the exchange of criminal justice information. The service publishes the electronic newsletter *Justice Information* twice each month.

National Institute of Justice (NIJ)
810 Seventh St. NW,
    Washington, DC20531
(202) 307-2942
Web site: www.ojp.usdoj.gov/nij

NIJ is the primary federal sponsor of research on crime and its control. It sponsors research efforts through grants and contracts that are carried out by universities, private institutions, and state and local agencies. Visitors to its Web site can find an overview of the Mafia and other organized crime groups.

Web Sites

ClevelandMob.com (www.clevelandmob.com)

This site is dedicated to news items and histories of Mafia activity in Ohio. It contains a photo gallery and downloads of news pieces.

Jerry Capeci's Gang Land (www.ganglandnews.com)

Capeci is a reporter best known for his "Gang Land" column in the *New York Daily News*. His site contains some of his columns as well as various Mafia histories, profiles, and news pieces.

Mafia International.com (http://glasgowcrew.tripod. com/index.html)

This Web site provides information about the Mafia's history, from its origins in Sicily through its spread into the United States. It also contains information on the Russian Mafia.

Rick Porrello's American Mafia (www.american mafia.com)

Porrello's site offers histories of the twenty-six Mafia families in America, links to various news articles, and a user forum for discussions of mob news.

Bibliography

Books

Joseph Bonanno, with Sergio Lalli — *A Man of Honor: The Autobiography of Joseph Bonanno.* New York: Simon & Schuster, 1983.

Jerry Capeci and Gene Mustain — *Gotti: Rise and Fall.* New York: Onyx, 1996.

Rick Cowan and Douglas Century — *Takedown: The Fall of the Last Mafia Empire.* New York: G.P. Putnam's Sons, 2002.

James O. Finckenauer and Elin J. Waring — *Russian Mafia in America: Immigration, Culture, and Crime.* Boston: Northeastern University Press, 1998.

Stephen R. Fox — *Blood and Power: Organized Crime in Twentieth-Century America.* New York: William Morrow, 1989.

James B. Jacobs, with Coleen Friel and Robert Radick — *Gotham Unbound: How New York Was Liberated from the Grip of Organized Crime.* New York: New York University Press, 1999.

James B. Jacobs, with Christopher Panarella and Jay Worthington — *Busting the Mob: United States v. Cosa Nostra.* New York: New York University Press, 1994.

Robert Lacey — *Little Man: Meyer Lansky and the Gangster Life.* Boston: Little, Brown, 1991.

Clare Longrigg

Mafia Women. London: Vintage, 1998.

Peter Maas

Underboss: Sammy the Bull Gravano's Story of Life in the Mafia. New York: HarperCollins, 1997.

Peter Maas

The Valachi Papers. New York: Putnam, 1968.

Sue Mahan, with Katherine O'Neil, eds.

Beyond the Mafia: Organized Crime in the Americas. Thousand Oaks, CA: Sage, 1998.

Gene Mustain and Jerry Capeci

Murder Machine: A True Story of Murder, Madness, and the Mafia. New York: Onyx, 1992.

Gerard O'Neill and Dick Lehr

The Underboss: The Rise and Fall of a Mafia Family. New York: PublicAffairs, 2002.

Nicholas Pileggi

Wiseguy: Life in a Mafia Family. New York: Pocket Books, 1985.

Rick Porrello

The Rise and Fall of the Cleveland Mafia: Corn, Sugar, and Blood. New York: Barricade Books, 1995.

Mario Puzo

The Godfather. New York: Signet, 1969.

Thomas A. Reppetto

American Mafia: A History of Its Rise to Power. New York: Henry Holt, 2004.

Robert Rudolph

The Boys from New Jersey: How the Mob Beat the Feds. New York: William Morrow, 1992.

Tim Shawcross

The War Against the Mafia: The Inside Story of a Deadly Struggle Against the Mob. New York: HarperCollins, 1995.

Ernest Volkman

Gangbusters: The Destruction of America's Last Great Mafia Dynasty. New York: HarperCollins, 1998.

Periodicals

James Barron

"Curtis Sliwa Fleeing City, Citing Fear of Mob Figures," *New York Times,* July 24, 2004.

Dan Barry

"Name Is Gotti, but Principle Is Peter," *New York Times,* November 20, 2004.

Geoffrey Colvin

"Business Has Become a Real Mob Scene," *Fortune,* November 24, 2003.

Richard Corliss and Simon Crittle

"The Last Don," *Time,* March 29, 2004.

Monica Davey

"In Mob Sweep, Feds Hope to Send Up the Clown," *New York Times,* April 26, 2005.

Alan Feuer

"Using an Informer, U.S. Agents Charge 45 in Mafia Crimes," *New York Times,* April 26, 2001.

Ingrid Walker Fields

"Family Values and Feudal Codes: The Social Politics of America's Twenty-First Century Gangster," *Journal of Popular Culture,* May 2004.

William
Glaberson

"Old Mobs Never Die, and Clichéd
but Brutal Methods Refuse to Fade
Away," *New York Times,* January 26,
2003.

Rick Hampton

"Gotti Dies with His Legacy in Ru-
ins," *USA Today,* June 11, 2002.

Jenny Johnston

"How the Dapper Don Was the Death
of the Mob; the Mafia Is History as
They Bury Godfather Gotti Today,"
Mirror (London), June 15, 2002.

John Lombardi

"The Dumbest Don," *New York,* January 17, 2005.

Jack Newfield

"Dumb-Dumb's Bullets," *New York,*
April 7, 2003.

William K. Rash-
baum and Joe
Schoenmann

"Detectives Used Badges to Kill for
the Mob, Indictments Say," *New York
Times,* March 11, 2005.

David Remnick

"Is This the End of RICO?" *New
Yorker,* April 2, 2001.

Lee Siegel

"The Attraction of Repulsion," *New
Republic,* December 13, 2004.

Time

"All in the Families," March 29, 2004.

Index

Albanese, Jay, 40, 42
Amuso, Vittorio "Vic," 18
Analyze This (film), 80
Anastasia, George, 43

Balancia, Louis, 65–66
Banana War, 10
Barnes, Leroy "Nicky," 19
Basciano, Vincent, 15
Bevacqua, Paul "Pauli Guns," 17
Bochte, Frank, 32, 33
Bonanno, Joe, 10
Bonanno family, 10, 15–16, 27
bookmaking, 44
    surveillance technology in
        crackdown on, 45–46, 48–50
Borsellino, Paolo, 71
Bruno, Angelo "Docile Don," 35,
    36–37
Busting the Mob (Jacobs), 33

Cacace, Joel "Joe Waverly," 16, 17
Calabrese, Nicholas, 34
Capeci, Jerry, 14, 15
Capone, Al, 8
Caponigro, Antonio "Tony Ba-
    nanas," 37
Caprio, Peter "the Crumb," 36
Castellano, Paul, 24
Centaro, Robert, 69
Chase, David, 83
Chicago, Mafia in, 8
    2005 indictments of, 30–34
Chicago Tribune (newspaper), 34
Chickara, James F., 75
Cirillo, Dominick "Quiet Dom,"
    18
CNN/Money, 72
Colombo family, 16–17, 27
Coppola, Francis Ford, 80, 83

Cosa Nostra, La, 10
    see also Mafia
Crea, Steven, 18

Daidone, Louis "Louie Bagels," 18
D'Arco, Alphonse "Little Al," 18
DeCavalcante, Simone "Sam the
    Plumber," 20
DeCavalcante family, 14, 19–20, 41
Defede, Joseph "Little Joe," 18
DeNapoli, Joseph, 19
Dentico, Lawrence "Little Larry,"
    18
DeRoss, John "Jackie," 16
De Stefano, George, 79
Di Caprio, Leonardo, 80
DiGregorio, Gaspar, 10

Electronic Privacy Information
    Center, 46
Evening Standard (newspaper), 22
Excellent Cadavers (Stille), 81, 82

Falcone, Giovanni, 71
Farace, Constabile "Gus," 63
Federal Bureau of Investigation
    (FBI), 29
    efforts of, against Mafia, 40–42
    under J. Edgar Hoover, 7, 8
films, Mafia portrayed in, 22, 80
Fitzgerald, Patrick, 34
Fourth Amendment, 53
Freeh, Louis, 40
Fuentes, Thomas, 41

Gambino family, 11, 14, 25, 27, 41
Garcia, Andy, 80
Gardell, Stephen E., 76, 77
Gelman, Norris, 51, 52

Genovese family, 17–18, 27
Gigante, Mario, 17–18
Gigante, Vincent "Chin," 17, 26
Gioeli, Thomas "Tommy Shots," 16–17
Giuffre, Antonio, 70
Giuliani, Rudolph, 22, 26
Godfather, The (film), 80, 83
GoodFellas (film), 23
Gotham Unbound: How New York City Was Liberated from the Clutches of Cosa Nostra (Jacobs), 81
Gotti, John, 11, 14, 21, 25
    funeral of, 22–23
Gotti, Peter, 25
Grasso, Piero, 70
Gravano, Salvatore, 12
Gravano, Sammy "the Bull," 24
Groppi, James, 85

Hart, Alan, 53
Heron, Matthew, 69–70, 71
Hoover, J. Edgar, 7, 9, 33, 40

Italian Americans
    Mafia as pop-culture expression of identity of, 84–85
    media stereotyping of, 83–84

Jacobs, James, 33, 81

Kael, Pauline, 84
Kallstrom, James, 66
Kaplan, David E., 39
Kennedy, Robert, 9, 40
Kirkpatrick, Thomas, 31

Labate, James S., 74, 76
Lansky, Meyer, 8
Las Vegas, Mafia in, 8, 11

Lombardo, Joseph "the Clown," 31, 32
Lucchese (Luchese) family, 10, 14, 18–19, 27
Lupo, Salvatore, 70

Madonna, Matthew, 19
Mafia
    decline in, 9–12, 68–69, 81–82
    early years of, 7–9
    as pop-culture expression of Italian-American identity, 84–85
    portrayal of, in films, 22, 80
    Sicilian
        growth of, 82–83
        link between American Mafia and, 70–71
Maloney, Andrew, 24
Mangano, Venero "Benny Eggs," 17
Marcantonio, Vito, 85
Marcello, James, 32
Massino, Joseph "Big Joey," 7, 15, 16, 26, 36
Mawn, Barry, 73, 78
Mazzarella, Darin, 55, 56–66
McAlary, Mike, 55
Merlino, Joseph "Skinny Joey," 36
Migliore, Aniello "Neil," 19
Miranda, Joseph, 20
Monastero, Stefano, 8
Morello, Celeste, 37
Morgenthau, Robert, 28
murders, mob-related, 31

Natale, Ralph, 36
New York
    culture of, Mafia in, 21–24
    Mafia families of, 11, 14, 27
        activities of, 28–29

securities-fraud scheme of, 72–78
Mafia in, 8, 81–82
media, portrayal of Mafia by, 24–25
New York Post (newspaper), 24

O'Donnell, Steven, 68
Omerta (Puzo), 80
omerta code, 7, 36
Operation Uptick, 73
Orena, Victor "Little Vic," 17
Outfit, the, 8–9

Paulson, Amanda, 30
Persico, Alphonse "Allie Boy," 26
Persico, Carmine "Junior," 16
Persico, Frank A. "Frankie," 26, 77
Petrucelli, Joey, 63
Petrucelli, John, Sr., 62–63
Petrucelli, Johnnie Boy, 61, 62, 63, 64
Philadelphia, Mafia in
decline of, 35–37
syndicates replacing, 37–38
Piazza, Salvatore, 74, 76
Pileggi, Nicholas, 23
Pirro, Jeanine, 66
Politan, Nicholas, 46, 51
Profaci, Joe, 10
Puzo, Mario, 80

Rabito, Anthony, 16
Racketeer Influenced and Corrupt Organizations (RICO) Act (1970), 11, 25, 30, 33, 39
Rametta, Sebastian, 75
Riggi, Giovanni "John," 19
Roane, Kit R., 35
Rotundo, Anthony, 19

Russo, Anthony, 16

Sacco and Vanzetti, 85
Saladino, Frank "Gumba," 31, 32
Savio, Mario, 85
Scarfo, Nicodemo D. "Little Nicky," 43, 46–48, 53
Schiro, Paul "the Indian," 31
Schweihs, Frank "the German," 32
Scoca, Vincent, 51
Seglem, Lee, 37
Siegel, Benjamin "Bugsy," 9
Sobel, David L., 46, 50, 53
Sopranos, The (TV series), 80–81, 83, 84
Spilotro, Anthony "the Ant," 31
Spilotro, Michael, 32
Stiles, Michael, 36
Stille, Alexander, 81, 82
Stropoli, Anthony, 77
surveillance technology, 43
in post-9/11 law enforcement, 51–53
privacy rights and, 50–51

Testa, Phil "Chicken Man," 37
Toccos family, 12
Tresca, Carlo, 85

Usborne, David, 21

Valachi, Joe, 11

Walker, Clarence, 67
Walker, Richard, 73, 76
White, Mary Jo, 66, 73
Wigler, Ronald, 46
Wolfson, Alan, 75

Zucconi, V., 81